Need a Miracle?

Need a Miracle?

Harald Bredesen
with
James F. Scheer

Fleming H. Revell Company
Old Tappan, New Jersey

Library of Congress Cataloging in Publication Data

Bredesen, Harald.
    Need a miracle?

    1. Miracles—Case studies. I. Scheer, James F., joint author. II. Title.
BT97.2.B67   231′.73   79-4599
ISBN 0-8007-0995-0

Contents

Preface

It was late when the two teenage sisters left the huge shopping complex—and so dark that they could hardly see the outline of their car, the only vehicle left in that section of the parking area.

Newspapers had featured all sorts of stories about muggings, rapes, and even brutal murders in shopping malls, so they cautiously glanced left and right, hurrying toward their car.

"It's creepy," whispered one of the girls.

"Don't I know?" responded the other.

Street traffic had subsided, and it was ominously quiet.

When they opened the car doors, two men jumped out from behind, shouting, "You're not going anywhere! You're going with us!"

Terrified, the girls scrambled into the car and clicked their door locks closed.

The driver turned on the car's ignition switch, and nothing happened, so she did it again. There was no response.

The men tried the doors. Quickly the girls joined hands in prayer.

"Dear God," pleaded the driver, "give us a miracle, in the name of Jesus!"

She turned on the switch again. This time the motor started. She shifted into gear and raced out of the parking lot, leaving the men behind.

Safe at home, the girls told their father about their frightening experience.

"I'm glad you're both safe. That's the main thing. But don't stay out so late again." Then he reflected for an in-

7

stant. "The car has never failed to start before. I'll check it
out tomorrow."

The next morning he raised the car's hood to examine the
starter, and he saw something that raised gooseflesh on his
arms: There was no battery!

This spine-tingling story was told to a nationwide TV
audience by Pastor Howard Conatser, of the Beverly Hills
Baptist Church, Dallas, Texas, and is typical of true hap-
penings reported throughout these pages.

Cases in *Need A Miracle?*—written as a handbook of
hope—are drawn from numerous sources: from my own life
and that of my collaborator, James F. Scheer; from reliable
persons I have known well; from individuals interviewed by
me and my collaborator; from persons who have appeared
on *Charisma,* the internationally distributed television program which I host for the Christian Broadcasting Network;
from this network's 700 Club programs; from Jim Bakker
on his worldwide PTL Club telecasts; from Thomas R.
Nickel's *Testimony* magazine; and public testimonies of
Diane Bringold, Michael Esses, ex-heavyweight boxing
champion George Foreman, Bud Godby, Carole Johnson,
William Converse Jones, Bengt Junvik, Patricia Martin,
Father John Medaris, Jan Opperman, Edith Schaeffer,
Demos Shakarian, president of the Full Gospel Business
Men's Fellowship International, Madame Bilquis Sheikh,
and Watson Spoelstra.

Dr. H. Richard Casdorph, Long Beach, California, personally supplied authentic information on miraculous healings.

Special thanks go to Carolyn Scheer for her innumerable
contributions to making the writing of this book possible.

                                                        HARALD BREDESEN

Need a Miracle?

1 Chance—Or Something More?

Do me a favor. Leave everything else
on the tape, but delete that one phrase:
"a bit of madness."

Were my ears playing tricks on me? I asked the man on the other end of the line to repeat himself.

"How would you like a congregation of twenty million people?"

"Who's going to give it to me?" I asked.

"I am. My name is Sack—John Sack. I'm senior producer for the CBS Walter Cronkite show, and we plan to come out with our TV crew to film a program to find out whether or not miracles still happen."

By this time, I had recovered my composure and invited him and his crew to the next miracle service at the historic First Reformed Church in Mount Vernon, New York.

Meanwhile, my wife was signaling me that she had the CBS–TV Religious Affairs Department on the other line. It turned out that they wanted to do something similar, but the Cronkite crew had beaten them to the draw.

After a day of filming in and around the church, John Sack, a man of Jewish heritage, but no faith, phoned. He told me, "Harald, I thought you'd like to see the film and hear the reactions of leading theologians we interviewed on the question, 'Do miracles actually happen?' "

Over the phone he read me several reactions of leading

theologians, one from Bishop Gerald Hamilton Kennedy, President of the United Methodist Church, and another from an Episcopal lay theologian whose name escapes me, even though I do remember what he said. "I'm all for this dimension. In our old-line churches, services are so structured, so stereotyped, cut and dried. Our overstuffed parishioners come in, sit down on their overstuffed pews, expecting nothing to happen, and they're never disappointed. But in the first-century church, it was different. There was excitement, ebullience, freedom, and spontaneity. There's a reason why our communion wine in the Episcopal church is still eighteen percent alcohol. After all, everyone is entitled to a bit of madness."

"John, do me a favor," I pleaded. "Leave everything else on the tape, but delete that one phrase: 'a bit of madness.' That could be offensive to the Holy Spirit."

"Sorry, old man. Now you're on my turf. 'A bit of madness' stays in."

This upset me, so I joined some friends in prayer, asking God to edit that tape.

Two days later, another man on the CBS team—a new Christian—got a phone call from John Sack. "Hey, Stu, come on down quick!"

Stu came running to the studio and found John holding a strip of shriveled film.

"What happened to your film?" asked Stu.

"Well, it's the strangest thing. Our film editor has been with us for many years. And in all that time he's never done a stupid thing like this. Somehow or other, while the film on the First Reformed Church was moving through the editing machine, he leaned over it with his brush, and a glob of glue slipped off."

"What was on that strip anyway?" Stu asked.

"Oh, just a phrase, '. . . a bit of madness,' " he replied. "But don't tell Harald. He'll think it's a miracle!"

2 Test Case

In this age of skepticism, I often hear people say, "But God isn't working miracles anymore." I've got news for them—good news . . . .

Do you believe in miracles?

Years ago, I didn't. Nobody on earth could have convinced me that such things still happened.

Well, nobody on earth did. It took God to do that, and He did it in a wonderful way.

I have never been the same since.

One of my jobs as a student pastor at Bethlehem Lutheran Church in Aberdeen, South Dakota, was to call on members who had strayed to an upstart church where, rumor had it, miracles were taking place.

I tracked down the strays, only to be dumbfounded with stories too far-out to believe: a baby dying of pneumonia had been instantaneously healed; a woman had been healed of a goiter, and a hopelessly cross-eyed man had thrown away his glasses and gone back to work healed.

I should have been delighted to discover that Jesus Christ "is the same yesterday, today, and forever," as the Scripture affirms in Hebrews 13:8, but instead I was very much upset. New truth is always upsetting, and this was particularly so, because, if it were true, it would mean that I would have to reevaluate so many of the statements that I had been taught from earliest childhood and I had taken at face value. One of these was that the age of miracles was past. I thought the best way for me to find out the truth was through a test case.

In our congregation there was a totally crippled arthritic, confined for eighteen years to her wheelchair. I wasn't going to make it easy for the Lord. In the church offices, I said, "Lord, if You heal today just as You did when You were on earth, prove it to me in Your Word. I'm going to take a Bible, plunk it down with my eyes closed, open it at random and put my finger on the page. In the verse my finger touches, I want You to tell me: Do You heal today, or don't You?"

When I opened my eyes and saw the verse, I was astonished. It was, "Bless the Lord, O my soul . . . Who forgiveth all thine iniquities; who healeth all thy diseases" (Psalms 103:1, 3).

I went to the woman's home and told her what had happened. "Do you want me to pray for you?" I asked.

"Oh, yes," she exclaimed.

I took out the bottle of oil to anoint her according to James 5:14: "Is any sick among you? let him call for the elders of the church; and let them pray over him, anointing him with oil . . . ."

And then I looked again at her hunched and grotesque figure. She struggled to fold her hands in prayer, but her grossly enlarged and distorted fingers could not obey. Finally, in resignation, she gave up and laid her hands in her lap.

My faith was growing smaller by the moment. In fact, it was already down to the size of a mustard seed. Then I remembered that Jesus had said that was all that was needed, provided I acted upon it.

I did.

The following day I went back with little expectancy, and

was met by a radiant woman, who said, "Pastor, last night, for the first time in eighteen years, I had absolutely no pain!"

In no time at all, the woman was up and around, taking care of her family.

God's cure of the woman's arthritis helped cure me of disbelief.

Some years later, when I was in Taiwan, I spoke on present day miracles to Madame Chiang Kai-shek's prayer group at the home of her chaplain. After a garden party there, I told the chaplain I was going back to the Grand Hotel. His daughter Lee asked if she could share the taxi with me.

I agreed. The breeze felt fresh through the open window of the cab, which careened across a narrow bridge. Suddenly I saw something red—a glowing cigarette butt from the window of an oncoming cab. Before I could dodge, the red hit the cornea of my eye, and I heard a sizzling sound.

Then I realized why God had sent this girl to ride with me, because she knew what to do instantly. She headed the cab toward the home of one of the two doctors in Taipei who practiced Western medicine.

He studied my eye carefully, and said, "You have sustained a severe burn of the cornea. I will scrape your eyeball, give you a sedative, and pack your eye. If the pain becomes too great during the night, call me."

The next morning, Sunday, I was supposed to speak in the nearby leprosarium, and a young couple, Pat and Bob Cummings, was to drive me there and sing. Down the corridor from them was an American, Creed Davis, who was in the immigration service. A stranger in Taipei, he was praying, "Lord, show me where I should go to church this morning."

He heard the Cummings softly rehearsing one of their songs as they walked down the corridor and approached them. "You must be Christians," he said.

They nodded.

"Yes. We're about to take Harald Bredesen to the leprosarium, where he is going to minister, and we are going to sing."

"Harald Bredesen!" he responded. "I know Harald."

So they came up to my room and found me flat on my back and in pain, with a huge patch over my eye.

"Let's lay hands on him and pray," said Pat and Bob.

That was what they did.

While they were praying for me, I fell asleep. Then they stopped praying and started to praise God in faith for my healing. When I awakened, there was absolutely no pain, swelling, or any redness to show that I had had a burn. When the doctor checked me out, he was amazed to discover absolutely no evidence that there had been a burn.

In this age of skepticism, I often hear people say, "But God isn't working miracles anymore."

I've got news for them—*good news*—God isn't working miracles any less.

Some breathtaking miracles have happened to me—not once, but many times. The hundreds of genuine miracles that I know about personally are not just physical healings, dramatic as they are. God is versatile. He can work dazzling miracles that cover the whole range of human experience. He can marvelously free us from any or all kinds of problems: the steel grip of bad habits or devastating and demoralizing addictions; life-threatening danger or hazards—in cities or rugged natural settings; physical, mental, and career limitations; emotional and financial despair or even disaster; and anything else.

Are you or your loved ones seemingly buried under an avalanche of problems too desperate and far beyond you to handle?

Have you tried everything, only to find that nothing

works? Is there no human way out? If not, there's something infinitely better: God's way, His perfect solution, His miracle-working power.

If you disagree, you might be interested in what God did for the following individuals who had already exhausted all human resources:

- A woman so crippled with rheumatoid arthritis that she couldn't dress herself or go to the bathroom without help
- A man with a crooked spinal column and ruptured discs who had been in a brace for thirty-eight years
- A baby with a waterhead and an inoperable tumor
- A man and wife so estranged that they never wanted to hear from or see each other again
- A woman whose health was being undermined by the very cigarettes she could not stop smoking
- An alcoholic who had lost everything, including hope
- A teenage boy hooked on heroin
- A homosexual who was soul sick because he had tried many times and failed to quit this practice
- A racing driver whose skull had been sheared open, pronounced dead by the track physician
- A businessman who had failed in every human effort to raise an instant $14 million to save his business and investors from financial disaster

Sound pretty hopeless?

All cases were until the individuals involved, their relatives, or friends reached out for a miracle.

There's nobody who, at some time, doesn't need a miracle.

If they don't occur in response to our prayers, the reasons can be numerous. Yet there is usually one major but little-recognized reason, one towering impediment: *ourselves.*

Some of us block the availability of miracles, or the

answers to *any* prayers, for that matter, by consciously or unconsciously thinking of God in too small terms, of considering Him in terms of our own human limitations.

What's a typical attitude? That of, "Who knows? Maybe He did work miracles in the past, but He's not doing it now!"

Anyone who says or thinks that probably needs a miracle to open his or her eyes to awe-inspiring events happening all over the world today.

God is still God—all-knowing and almighty. He is still a full-service God, not a limited-service God. And He is available to hear and answer sincere prayers made in faith.

One of them could be yours!

3 _Cures for the Incurable_

> Suddenly the minister felt as if chips of ice had been sprinkled on his back, and his spinal column began moving, straightening out, as if under the guidance of an expert hand.

Does this chapter title, "Cures for the Incurable" seem contradictory? If diseases, ailments, or individuals are incurable, how can they possibly be cured?

The answer is simple: God doesn't know they're incurable.

Perhaps you have a physical disability so tenacious and long enduring that you think it will be with you as long as you live: arthritis; a back problem; a deformed limb; paralysis; blindness; deafness; multiple sclerosis; a heart or artery ailment; today's most feared disease, cancer; or some other ailment which baffles the best medical minds.

Doctors arbitrarily tell us that certain conditions are incurable, because they know the limitations of their profession. What they don't always admit is that God has no limitations. If He could work the miracles of creating us, He can also cure us.

Until recently, physicians could shrug off claims of miracles without bothering to check into them, but now a member of their own profession is making in-depth inquiries into them.

One of the foremost scientific investigators of such claims is Dr. H. Richard Casdorph, of Long Beach, California. Both my coauthor, James F. Scheer, and I have discussed this matter with the doctor, who devoted several years to researching cases which he found to be prime examples of almost unbelievable, supernatural cures.

Highly respected among his peers, Dr. Casdorph has distinguished himself in his profession. He served for four and one-half years on the staff of the world renowned Mayo Clinic in Rochester, Minnesota. During his career, he has published seventy-two articles in scientific journals and written a medical textbook, *Treatment of the Hyperlipidemic States,* that is standard in many medical schools and physicians' offices. He has been chief of the department of internal medicine at Long Beach Community Hospital.

Curious and fascinated by reported healings, mainly through the Christian ministry of the late Kathryn Kuhlman, Dr. Casdorph determined to study as many cases as time would permit from his demanding practice, checking doctors and surgeons who had treated or operated upon these patients, scrutinizing "before" and "after" X rays, medical records, and interviewing the patients themselves. He went even a step farther, enlisting a board of outstanding and impartial physicians to agree or disagree with his observations, through examinations and analysis of all available data in each case: written reports, angiograms, brain scans, biopsy slides, pyelograms, total-body scans, and comparative X rays.

When the board finished, their votes backed the findings of Dr. Casdorph. They could find no physical reasons for complete cures from hopeless conditions which should have led to worsening invalidism and, in most instances, death.

Dr. Casdorph followed up on the supposedly healed to make sure that they remained healthy. When this proved to be true, Dr. Casdorph compiled ten of the most unusual and diverse cases and included them in an arresting book, *The Miracles*.

These ranged from chronic rheumatoid arthritis, malignant brain tumor, and arteriosclerotic heart disease to massive gastrointestinal hemorrhage with shock, multiple sclerosis, osteoporosis of the whole spine, and cancer of the kidney. Let's briefly consider the facts in three of the cases.

Normally rheumatoid arthritis is a condition that changes only for the worse. If it does improve by itself or due to medical treatment, the improvement is gradual.

Mrs. Elfrieda Stauffer, of La Mesa, California, had become so crippled with chronic rheumatoid arthritis that she could neither dress herself nor go to the bathroom without help. For many years her ability to move around decreased and her pain increased.

On the Sunday of January 14, 1974, she attended a Kathryn Kuhlman service at the Shrine Auditorium in Los Angeles. Her pain was almost unbearable.

When Miss Kuhlman asked everyone with pain in the shoulder to step into the aisle, Mrs. Stauffer hesitated at first. Sure, she had pain there, but why single out only that area? She ached everywhere. How could she possibly rise and step out into the aisle? She tried to move in her seat and couldn't believe what she felt.

The pain had gone from the shoulder, wrists, knees, ankles—all parts of her body!

Almost in tears of gratitude to God, she rose to her feet and walked.

"It was the first time since I can't remember when that I had no pain," she admits.

Today the woman who couldn't walk, dress, or go to the bathroom on her own, wears high-heel shoes, gardens, does housework, and plays a good game of tennis.

Medical doctors found the case of sixty-five-year-old Marvin K. Bird, of Huntington Beach, California, impossible. He had been hospitalized seventeen times in sixteen years for a severe heart condition—total occlusion (blockage) of one coronary artery and 50 percent obstruction of two other coronary blood vessels. Doctors recommended a coronary bypass operation to save his life.

"No," replied Bird. "I don't think I could live through that."

It was a serious question whether Marvin Bird was going to live either way. His chest pain was excruciating, as if the weight of an army tank were upon him. To alleviate the torture, he tried a succession of drugs: nitroglycerin, Darvon, Percodan, and then injected narcotics. Nothing helped him. Now he was sentenced to the rest of his life in bed. He could not gather enough strength even to turn over.

One night Bird experienced an unforgettable dream. With unbelievable realism, he watched as his dead father and brother-in-law came over a hill toward him and gestured for him to come with them.

This dream and his hopeless condition were enough to tell him his earthly time was short.

Soon after this, his wife insisted that he attend a Kathryn Kuhlman service at the Shrine Auditorium in Los Angeles. On the night before, he had a second dream, in which he helped a relative from Iowa find an apartment. The number on its door was 315—a prophetic number.

On Sunday, November 19, 1972, Marvin Bird, dulled with pain-killing pills, sat in a wheelchair next to his wife in the packed-to-capacity shrine. Mrs. Bird suddenly felt a warmth in her head, drifting down through her entire body. The next thing she knew, Maggie Hartner, a Kuhlman aide, said there was a healing in the area and asked Marvin to stand up.

No one was more surprised than Bird when he was able to obey. He knew he was completely cured, because he felt great. Then he sat down, and, as he did so, he glanced at his watch. The time? Exactly 3:15 P.M., the same number as that on the door of the apartment he had found for the Iowa relative in his dream.

Along with heart and artery ailments, various forms of cancer are the most fear-inspiring and usually unyielding diseases of our time. But no human condition can resist God's healing light, as dramatically illustrated by another case validated by Dr. Casdorph.

During March of 1970, Marie Rosenberger, forty-four-year-old wife of Herman Rosenberger, an ordained minister and Dean of Students of the Life Bible College in Southern California, experienced severe headaches, diarrhea, and drastic loss of weight, leading to in-depth tests and, finally, brain surgery.

Although the surgeon was able to cut away a golf-ball-size tumor from the left temporal lobe, he was unable to remove all the malignancy without irreparable damage to the patient.

Marie Rosenberger underwent cobalt therapy, starting on May 13. After a brief gain, she rapidly deteriorated to a point where she was unable to read, write, or speak for a year. Another examination revealed that the tumor was growing back. The neurosurgeon said there were only two ways to go to save her: surgery or chemotherapy.

Herman Rosenberger decided on a third way: prayers to God. With his wife back at home again, he enlisted prayer power from several sources: the Angelus Temple Prayer Tower, the Oral Roberts University Prayer Tower, Kathryn Kuhlman, and the churches in which Rosenberger had pastored. He didn't stop there. He assembled the whole family for an all-night prayer session. Around midnight, Rosenberger, exhausted, rested for a few hours, resuming prayer at 2:00 A.M. This time, however, the prayer changed from one in customary language to a prayer in the Holy Spirit—in foreign tongues which he did not understand and, in English, a torrent of Scriptures on divine healing.

In the midst of this prayer glow, he got a clear message from the Holy Spirit of God: "Marie will be well from the top of her head to the soles of her feet."

A vision flooded Rosenberger's mind—a picture of Marie's tumor disintegrating and disappearing. Immediately Herman shared his knowledge with the others.

On that evening the family assembled with Marie for prayer to Jesus, whose presence all sensed, and Marie felt a popping in her head and the opening of her ear.

Rosenberger exclaimed, "In Jesus' name, the tumor is gone. One of these mornings, you will need no medication."

On the next morning, Rosenberger's divinely motivated prophecy came true. She was able to stop medication, and, soon after that, could speak and see again.

After a month, the Rosenbergers visited her neurosurgeon, who found her much improved, asking what medication she was now on.

Rosenberger at first held back the information that they had never picked up the prescription he had phoned to their pharmacy.

All right, if she wasn't on medicine he had prescribed, what was she taking?

Herman shook his head. "None. Prayer is our medicine."

Mystified, the surgeon told the Rosenbergers to keep on doing whatever they were doing. Six months later, the neurosurgeon's answer became even more optimistic. He had no hesitation about saying that the change was obviously the answer to prayers.

Marie began to assume full duties as a housewife and companion and was pronounced cured. Yet occasionally, her words would come out garbled, because some of the dominant temporal lobe of her brain, which controls such things, had been removed to eliminate malignancy.

When Dr. Casdorph interviewed the Rosenbergers, he had subtly suggested that he thought that Herman was protecting Marie from situations where she would have to speak and become embarrassed from her speech defect.

"Marie really should be getting out to tell people the marvelous miracle God has worked in her life," he said.

A few months later, Dr. Casdorph was invited to join Dean Rosenberger and his wife, to speak at the Life Bible College chapel.

"I was stunned at the change in Marie," he states. "She seemed in radiant health and spoke flawlessly. It was hard for me to believe that so much good had happened to her in such a short time."

Dean Rosenberger then told Dr. Casdorph that a beautiful little miracle followed the big one. "I had been overprotecting Marie," he admitted. "I urged her to go out as frequently as the Lord wanted her, and give her Christian testimony. The more she spoke, the better her speech became. Additionally, at meetings where she and I spoke, people who requested our prayers were healed."

God, true to His Word, through the Holy Spirit, had healed Marie from the top of her head to the soles of her feet.

Probably the most astonishing miracles are instantaneous healings of long-enduring physical disabilities.

Reverend Ambrose La Velle, pastor of St. Luke's Methodist Church in Maryville, Illinois, would agree, because just such a miracle happened to him at a Kathryn Kuhlman service in 1973. In an instant, he was cured of a crippling condition that had kept him imprisoned in a cumbersome steel-and-leather brace for thirty-eight years: a crooked spinal column and a ruptured disc that had worn paper thin.

So many thousands packed the auditorium that Pastor La

Velle felt lost among them, until suddenly Miss Kuhlman pointed at him, and he knew for sure she meant him, for she announced, "Your crooked spinal column and ruptured disc have been healed."

Suddenly the minister felt as if chips of ice had been sprinkled on his back, and his spinal column began moving, straightening out, as if under the guidance of an expert hand. Within seconds he was able to remove his brace—a process that usually took him an hour—walk to the stage, and bend, touching the floor.

"That was something I hadn't been able to do since I was seventeen," he says gratefully.

His surprised physician examined him, took X rays, and confirmed the healing.

Another remarkable thing then took place. He recalled Miss Kuhlman having predicted, "Healings will now happen in your church."

And they have. Healing services are now a regular part of Pastor La Velle's weekly church activities.

A long-time cancer patient, Captain John LeVrier, chief of the traffic department of the Houston police, had been given the grim news by three physicians that his only outlook was death.

Already, in 1968, inoperable cancer of the pelvic area had sent wild growth to his spine. Some fifty-eight cobalt treatments through 1970 could not stop the spread. Although a skeptic who considered miracles and those who allegedly had a part in them "phonies," Captain LeVrier, in February 1971 dragged his energyless and pain-filled body to a Los Angeles Kuhlman service with a what-have-I-got-to-lose? attitude.

He remembers Miss Kuhlman saying, "God, I know You can heal today, just as You always could. I now ask in Jesus' name that You heal."

Captain LeVrier then became aware that Miss Kuhlman

was pointing directly at him and asking him to stand and claim his healing.

Still a doubter, the captain rose. A charge of new energy shot through him like a high-voltage current, and, wonder of wonders, all the pain was gone.

Two cancer specialists examined him and found no sign of cancer. One of them, Dr. Lowell S. Miller, of Anderson Hospital and Tumor Institute of Houston, states that there is no spontaneous remission from the kind of cancer Le-Vrier had. Occasionally this type of cancer will slow its pace, but it will not disappear, explains Dr. Miller. In the case of LeVrier, X rays taken in 1970 showed definite terminal cancer. Those taken after his return to Texas showed no sign of cancer.

Captain LeVrier now preaches faith, and he gives the glory and thanks for his healing to the living God.

Healings of so-called incurable conditions do not always occur instantaneously. Former U.S. Army Major General John Medaris will vouch for that.

Suffering from excruciating bone cancer and given a year to live by his doctors, General Medaris, who had been head of the Army's space and rocket program in its most productive years, received the laying on of hands, with prayer, from Mrs. Virginia Lively, of Belle Glade, Florida, and felt immediate improvement. In less than two years, all trace of the cancer had disappeared. A housewife who has held healing services for almost a generation, Mrs. Lively claims that the healing power comes from God, through Jesus Christ.

Overwhelmed by the experience, Medaris retired from his military career, went into Christian ministry, and is now Father Medaris, an Episcopal priest.

Often miraculous healings are God's instruments to bring unbelievers to Him. Certainly this was so with Watson

Spoelstra, former sportswriter for the *Detroit News*.

A hard drinker, a hell raiser and someone who didn't believe in or have time for God, Spoelstra went through a remarkable transformation over a period of several days.

After covering the Detroit Lions–Cleveland Browns football game and writing coverage, Watson Spoelstra drove home, finding his wife distressed over their eighteen-year-old daughter, a freshman at the University of Michigan.

"Ann was lying on the bathroom floor when we came home. She's got a splitting headache and an upset stomach and is in bed."

The Spoelstra family physician, Dr. Edward Draues, gave Ann medicine, but it failed to alleviate her headache or nausea.

New Year's Day's Rose Bowl game didn't interest Ann. Neither did a big broiled steak—her favorite food. Spoelstra reported this and her persistent headaches and nausea to the doctor, who immediately had her rushed to Providence Hospital.

A neurosurgeon, Dr. George R. Granger, called in as a consultant, said preliminary indications were that a blood vessel in her brain had broken. The doctor offered little hope. Ann received the last rites of the church.

Watson and Jean Spoelstra alternated eighteen- to twenty-hour shifts with their daughter in room 298.

Periodically Ann would ask her parents, "What's wrong with me?"

It was hard to conceal their tears and pessimism from her. Then Ann was wheeled away for tests, including an arteriogram. While she was gone, the Spoelstras went into the quiet hospital chapel.

Then and there Watson Spoelstra made a deal with God.

"Listen, God," he said. "I want to make a deal with You. I've never paid much attention to You. You must be here in this chapel. Listen, God. Do something about Ann, and I'll let You do something with me."

Nothing seemed to happen at the time, but now Spoelstra had made a move toward God, and, so it is said, God would move toward him.

Watson and Jean hurried back to learn results of Ann's tests from the neurosurgeon, who said that Ann's hemorrhage was caused by an imperfect connection between an artery and vein in the right frontal part of the brain.

"It's a birth malformation," said the doctor.

An operation could be hazardous, but waiting could be, too. It would take a miracle, but scar tissue could possibly form a new and satisfactory connection.

They decided to wait. Already Spoelstra had made his deal for a miracle with God.

And God kept His part of the bargain. Ann's headaches disappeared, and she became famished. She recovered fully.

Spoelstra followed through on his part of the bargain, too. He began "reading the cover off the Bible," lost his desire for alcohol, joined a church, and eventually began working with the Bill Glass ministry, which brought Sunday-morning devotional services to professional football and baseball players before games on the road. For four years he told his Christian conversion story in churches, with Glass, who, by then, had added national crusades to his ministry for bringing the message of Jesus Christ to thousands.

In 1973 Watson Spoelstra made an early retirement from the *Detroit News* and withdrew with regret from the Bill Glass program to head Baseball Chapel Incorporated.

As Spoelstra looks back over the years of his life, the best deal he ever made was in the chapel at Providence Hospital.

"Providence," says Spoelstra. "What an appropriate name!"

No one can tell Watson Spoelstra and others mentioned in this chapter that God's promises of healing in the Bible are just so many lifeless and empty words.

Yet modern churches teach that such miracles are not for

today. They write off miracles as of the distant past. They intimate that God went out of the healing business in the first century A.D. It is perhaps fortunate that God has not visited these churches in recent decades to learn this bad news.

Although sanitized interpretations of the Bible have done their best to reduce God to man's image and likeness, millions in congregations throughout the world continue to pray to a living, loving, eternal, and omnipotent God. And their faith and prayers still bring desired results.

4 *"Impossible" Cures Instantly*

"The mass is gone . . . . We don't
know what has happened. All we know
is that she has been healed."

A shock! That's exactly what Dr. William Standish Reed, of Tampa, Florida, got when he casually mentioned to another physician that patients could get great healing benefits if their doctors prayed for them.

"I don't know why we should pray," replied the physician. "What do we have ministers for?"

Dr. Reed knows why. For many years, he has seen prayer work miracles after medicines and the scalpel had failed. When he talks about prayer and the medical profession, he has the credentials for speaking authoritatively about both.

He is a member of the American Board of Surgery, the Christian Medical Society, and the Surgical Teaching Staff of Tampa General Hospital, as well as Chief of Surgery at St. Elizabeth's Hospital and University Community Hospital, and an active Episcopal layman.

"We've created beautiful hospitals, sterile as they can be, and put a little chapel there in the periphery that no sick person can even get into," he says. "It's usually the size of a broom closet. It's only a gesture to a bygone era when we believed in God in hospitals. Then we discourage nurses from praying . . . . We're a Christian land, but we practice atheism; it's as if God weren't there.

"If the average doctor believed in prayer, he'd pray . . . . When the patient is sick or in pain, the nurse materializes and gives a hypodermic in the posterior and leaves. Maybe all that's needed is a little kindness, a caress, or a moment of prayer.

"But we have created these fantastically sterile institutions, making them totally devoid of spirit and almost devoid of mind. We've mechanized to the point where the warmth, the love, and care that a human being requires is lost."

Is the vast medical profession ready to add prayer to its arsenal against disease and injury? Probably not yet, despite the steadily increasing membership in the small but vigorous Christian Medical Society and prayer action by a sprinkling of independents.

However, at least the profession is opening up enough to listen to information about prayer and miracles.

While it makes scientific sense to probe deeply into all available data and medical records before admitting the possibility of a miracle healing, scientists should not pooh-pooh this avenue of healing before initiating a thorough investigation. Many men explain away all possible miracles with the usual three lines of patter: "It was probably a pychosomatic condition. When the person's mental attitude changed, the condition cleared up." Or, "It was a wrong diagnosis. The patient didn't actually have the ailment claimed." Or even, "Instantaneous remission. It would have cleared up by itself."

Today, more than ever, physicians are cooperating with patients to make office records and X rays available for review and study by legitimate investigators. So a great deal more hard evidence now exists to prove that many claimed miracles are real miracles. In fact, the medical profession itself is bending enough to consider alternative methods of healing.

Not long ago, the International Academy of Parapsychology and Medicine invited Olga Worrall, who for many years had directed the Healing Clinic at Baltimore's Mount Washington Methodist Church, to take the platform before four hundred physicians at Stanford University.

Ten "incurable" patients of the doctors—those who had failed to respond to every known treatment—were brought to her for healing by God's power.

Mrs. Worrall laid hands upon them, and, in seven cases, the afflictions regressed before the eyes of the amazed group.

Doctors are also confounded by healings through the Christian ministry of Ted Whitesell.

A former eminently successful Alhambra, California, insurance man, Whitesell gave up elegant cars and memberships in prestigious country and beach clubs to become a full-time Christian worker, traveling on whatever continent God calls him.

His healing ministry began many years ago when his daughter was stung by a hornet. Her hand swelled, and she was crying with pain. Then he laid hands on her, and instantly the swelling went down and the pain left.

Since then Whitesell has circled the globe eight times, conducting healing services in Australia, New Zealand, Indonesia, Jamaica, Hong Kong, the Philippine Islands, the Bahamas, and England.

Whitesell, in his early seventies, has brought God's healing to an estimated thirty thousand individuals, although, "I don't keep score."

Wherever a church needs him to conduct healing services, he goes, accepting only travel and living expenses from donations. Not only have members of congregations been healed of arthritis, blindness, deafness, heart and artery ailments, colitis, and cancer, churches have been healed of disbelief and spiritual sterility.

Once Ted Whitesell held two healing sessions a week at the Red Room of Algemac's restaurant in Glendale, California. William McElroy, owner–manager of the eatery, told me what happened when word got around that all sorts of healings were taking place there: "People read an article about Brother Ted by religion editor Russell Chandler in the *Los Angeles Times,* and this place was packed. You couldn't get into our parking lot or find a place to park on the street for miles around." The room has since been renamed the Brother Ted Room.

Concerning one part of his healing ministry, Whitesell says, "Almost eighty percent of back problems are caused by uneven length of legs."

In a case like this, Whitesell usually works in the following way. He sits in a chair, opposite the seated person, holding his or her heels in his hands, closing his eyes, and praying. This results in uneven-length legs equalizing.

Once McElroy witnessed a rare miracle in Whitesell's ministry. A person came to Whitesell with one leg nine inches longer than the other as a result of an auto accident.

"He no sooner touched the young man than the legs equalized in length before our eyes.

"Once I went to radio station KGIL in the San Fernando Valley with Brother Ted. After he was interviewed, he fielded questions and prayer requests from listeners by phone. One woman wanted help for incurable eczema she had had for years. The station manager, sitting nearby and listening intently, also had eczema. Ted had hardly finished praying when the woman came on the phone again, crying with joy. Her eczema was gone. So was that of the station manager!"

Like others who call upon the healing power of Jesus for miracles, Whitesell occasionally runs into derisive skeptics. In London, while he was laying hands on sick individuals, a newspaper reporter and a photographer who had come to cover the story decided he was a phony.

"This bloke probably plants stooges in the audience and then claims to heal them," the photographer said in a loud stage whisper that Whitesell and all the others around couldn't help hearing.

On impulse, Whitesell turned toward the two, immediately noticing that one of the photographer's eyes continuously twitched.

"How long have you had that twitch?" Whitesell asked.

Embarrassed, as many in the room glanced at him, the photographer hesitantly replied, "For years."

"Would you like to get rid of it for good?" Whitesell asked.

The man nodded; Whitesell laid his hand over the fluttering eye and prayed.

"It is gone," said Whitesell in faith. "In the name of Jesus Christ, it is gone."

And it was.

"I can't believe it," the photographer kept repeating.

Also overcome with amazement, the reporter made an admission to Whitesell, "We were intending to give you a few short paragraphs, but, after this, man, you're going to get on the front page, with pictures." And he did.

Whitesell smiled on the inside, for he knew that God uses the most confirmed skeptics to spread His message to the world.

Less a skeptic than someone who felt he could take or leave God, Dr. Charles Woodhouse learned what Ted Whitesell already knew: God uses miracles to call attention to Himself and the Kingdom of heaven.

A Harvard University graduate and a former orthopedic surgeon at Tufts University, Dr. Woodhouse now in private practice, appeared on *Charisma,* a Christian Broadcasting Network television program which I host, and told millions of listeners a fascinating story.

During most of his life, he had attended church regularly: every Christmas Day and Easter Sunday. He had a great deal of confidence in himself and felt he was a good man because of the things he could do.

"I would point to children who walked, people who lived, to the good works I had done, to justify myself," he explained.

Then suddenly circumstances made him feel helpless.

His lovely, two-year-old daughter, Heather, developed epileptiform seizures. Electroencephalograms were made. She was put on the latest medicines for this condition and was getting the best possible consultations from a pediatrician, but she was still having seizures. There was nothing Dr. Woodhouse could do, nothing more he could buy that would help. There was nowhere he could turn, or so he thought, until his wife suggested turning to God.

"Martha turned to God, and I went along with her," he told me. "We heard of a doctor, Bill Reed, who was going to speak in my father-in-law's church.

"I looked him up in the medical directory and found he was a board-certified surgeon, as I am. He was on a faculty and had written some papers.

"He looked perfectly normal. Yet there was something about him that I couldn't understand or explain at the time. Bill Reed anointed Heather with oil and prayed for her, and my little daughter stopped having seizures."

Dr. Woodhouse concluded that Bill Reed's actions and prayers had worked the miracle!

"So I began to read the Bible regularly, because that was Bill Reed's textbook for surgery. In the Bible it said if you laid hands on the sick in Jesus' name, you could heal them," he explained.

Dr. Woodhouse decided to try it. He went to the hospital and selected patients with various types of ailments and laid hands on them and prayed. Each one was healed.

"Three or four weeks after that, I attended a Full Gospel Business Men's meeting, and I don't know what happened to me. I started to cry. I'd never before cried in my life. The Lord was speaking to me.

"I began to be ashamed of the junk in my life. I couldn't stand the burden of it and did exactly what the Bible tells you to do: ask Jesus to forgive you. I didn't believe it would work, but it did.

"Then I realized that the purpose of Heather's healing was to announce the Kingdom of God."

God's purpose remains the same in Dr. Woodhouse's continuing healing ministry, as this case illustrates.

"In a local high-school football game, a player was injured and came in with a badly shattered fracture and dislocation of the ankle, which is not easy to deal with. It is the kind of fracture in which you have to reduce the dislocation first and then wait until the swelling goes down and put pins in, in order to hold this difficult type of fracture together before an operation.

"I pray with all my patients before surgery. I don't dare touch a knife without asking God first. When I got the boy up in surgery that evening, I prayed a prayer that seemed to be right: 'Lord Jesus, set this fracture so that I don't have to operate next Thursday.' After doing that, I asked myself, *What am I praying? You just can't set these fractures without an operation.*

"I felt the ankle, reduced the dislocation, thought I had it in the right place, and said 'All right, let's take an X ray.' We took it, and you could see the three fracture lines, and they were set—perfectly set, instead of having to be operated on," he stated.

The reason for the accident and for God's healing came to light the next day.

"I made ward rounds, and there was this boy with his family. A couple of other patients were in nearby beds within hearing distance, too." Dr. Woodhouse turned to the boy and said, "Remember that prayer I prayed with you . . .?" Before the boy could react, the father, who didn't have the patience for talk about something as seemingly impractical as prayer, interrupted, "Are you going to operate next Thursday?"

Dr. Woodhouse again addressed the boy, "Do you remember that prayer I prayed?"

The boy brightened with the recollection and replied, "Yes, doctor, you prayed so that the fracture would be set and you wouldn't have to operate."

Dr. Woodhouse was delighted to announce that the ankle had set and there would be no operation.

"That's the kind of God I know," he told the group. "I don't know what you know about God, but I know the kind of God that you can ask things like that."

Dr. Woodhouse told me the whole point of what had happened. People are healed, as Luke indicated—not for the healing but to prove that Jesus is who He says He is.

A person who knows from experience that Luke's statement is correct is a distinguished American jurist, Judge Kermit Bradford, of Atlanta, Georgia, a healing channel of God.

All of the miracle healings in which he has been involved show God to be very much alive, active, and willing to draw attention to Himself and His efforts for the benefit of mankind. However, one in particular stands out in his mind. The incident generated local, then state and national newspaper publicity, through no effort on the judge's part.

A woman from Waycross, Georgia, someone he did not know, phoned him one morning as he was about to go on the bench.

"Judge, I have a little child that's dying from a brain tumor. And a lady here in town tells me you pray for people. I'm on my way to Atlanta to Eggleston Hospital to have them operate on my child's brain. Is there any way I can see you before I go?"

"Yes," responded the judge, "Bring the baby down to the courthouse so that we can pray."

She arrived with her eighteen-month-old daughter "hanging over her shoulder like a sack of salt." The baby's face was almost a sickly green in color.

Judge Bradford was surprised to observe that the child had a large waterhead.

The mother hurriedly explained that her baby had already been operated on twice, and that the doctor had told her a third operation could mean death.

The judge explained to her that no man can heal, but that God can heal through men.

"I laid my hands on the little child's head and prayed that God would loose her from this," he said.

"She left, and I mounted the bench and forgot all about it, because these things become a way of life, and you don't catalogue them.

"So the next morning about nine-thirty, the telephone rang. It was this young lady, who told me, 'Judge, would you like to know what happened after I left?'

" 'What happened?' "

" 'We raced down to the hospital with her. When they

saw that she was near death, they rushed her to the operating room. An hour passed, two hours, and three hours passed, and I began to pace the room.

" 'I knew something terrible had happened, or that she was dead. All of a sudden, the doctor walked out of the room with his operating jacket and mask on.

" 'Don't tell me she's dead, doctor!' I pleaded.

" ' "No, she's not dead. For three hours, we've been examining her. We took the previous X rays showing the mass on her brain, and then we made another X ray, and the mass wasn't there. We knew that was an error, and we sent her back to have another one made. That was in error, too. We had three made. We had a spinal tap made, but nothing was wrong. Then we had the whole staff up there to tap her from the top of the head to the bottom of her feet.

" ' "And for three hours we've been trying to work on her before we go into her brain. The mass is gone, and surely her head has begun to shrink down from a waterhead to normal. We don't know what has happened. All we know is that she has been healed." ' "

The doctor asked to have the baby brought back in four months for a checkup. For four years, the mother has been bringing in the child every four months, and she's still perfect.

The child's father, editor of the Waycross newspaper, featured the miracle in boxcar letters on the front page: JUDGE PRAYS FOR DAUGHTER, AND SHE'S HEALED IN HIS CHAMBERS.

God's healing covers the full spectrum of human diseases and disabilities. No ailment that anyone has can resist His power. It is no harder for Him to cure cancer than a cold.

But don't make the mistake of thinking that His miracle-working ends with physical conditions. It covers the full spectrum of human functions and activities.

Anything and everything that's wrong with you and me—unbreakable habits and addictions, emotional, mental, personality, marital, and financial problems—are all easy for Him to correct.

But first we have to believe He can, and second we have to give Him a chance.

5 *How to Break Bad Habits*

> "I had smoked for 35 years, five packs a day . . . . I lit the first cigarette, and then all were lighted from the previous one . . . . Six years ago, the Lord dealt with this problem in a beautiful, simple way . . . ."

You can quit any habit that has made you a slave!

Yes, *any* habit: coffee drinking, overeating, smoking, alcohol, or narcotics.

Others have broken the cold, steely grip of the most harmful and tenacious habits and addictions by a simple yet miraculous means available to everyone.

It can happen to you as it has to many persons I know and know about.

For one, James F. Scheer had a seemingly harmless addiction to coffee, which proved to be harmful. On four to five cups a day, he began to experience a high degree of nervousness, irritability, trembling, deep fatigue, agitation, and insomnia.

A Christian who, through prayer, turns to God for answers, one night Jim woke from a fitful sleep and saw a vision. At the same time, he was part of the vision. His large, off-white coffee mug with the letter *J* in black came before his eyes. Then a white, semitransparent porcelain hand clasped its palm and fingers over the top of the cup, as if forbidding him to drink.

Mentally, he asked, "Are You telling me not to drink coffee· anymore?"

Although he heard no reply, a strong impression came to him that the answer was *yes*.

Another question came to mind, "And if I don't quit . . . ?"

Suddenly he felt himself rise up, and saw himself on the bed—immobile, gray, and dead.

His prayers to end the twenty-year habit were answered. He has not had coffee for more than two years and has lost both the desire for it and the previous symptoms.

Since then, he has learned from various research studies that the caffeine in three cups of coffee equals the amount of stimulant doctors administer when a person's heart has stopped beating; that coffee increases the rate of heartbeat and blood pressure; that black coffee stimulates production of gastric juices more than any other beverage (it is forbidden by doctors to patients with gastric ulcers); it depletes vitamin B_1 from the system, a vitamin essential for mental and emotional health; and can produce symptoms often mistaken for anxiety neurosis.

A heavy cigarette smoker in one of my congregations needed no vision to tell her that she had to quit. Her doctor laid it right out: "Stop immediately, or you're going to die!"

What frightened her was that she couldn't quit. She came to me in desperation, and we prayed together. Several weeks later I saw her again. She smiled radiantly, saying, "Frankly, I was a skeptic. After I left you, I went home and, without conscious thought, picked up a cigarette and started to raise it to my lips. Then a strange thing happened. My arm stopped and, no matter how I tried, I couldn't finish the act. The smell of tobacco began to make me feel ill."

That was four years ago, and she has never again smoked.

Frances Gardner Hunter's experience in quitting was even more exciting.

"I had smoked for 35 years and had got to the point where I had to buy a carton of cigarettes every day, for I smoked five packs per day," she writes in *Testimony* magazine.

"I was working 16 to 18 hours a day, and I used only one match. I lit the first cigarette, and then all the rest were lighted from the previous one, for I was never without a cigarette. Six years ago, the Lord dealt with this problem in a beautiful, simple way, and I have never had the desire for a cigarette from that day to this."

Frances' secret? She gave herself to Jesus and got a new life in accordance with the Scripture: "Therefore if any man be in Christ, he is a new creature: old things are passed away; behold, all things are become new" (2 Corinthians 5:17).

In my various church and television ministries in the United States and Canada, I have learned that human methods for trying to break addictions usually bring only temporary success. We tend to deal with the symptoms, trying to change one area of our lives, rather than with the underlying causes. This is true of any addiction: coffee, overeating, smoking, alcohol, or hard drugs. A superficial or partial commitment usually brings only partial results. A total commitment like Frances Gardner Hunter's is a *must!*

When we turn our entire lives over to God, we not only shed old, negative habits, but old, incomplete, and unhappy lives, and we gain new habits and bright, new lives, free from past enslavements.

We sometimes regard certain habituations—tobacco, alcohol, and, especially, hard drugs—as the most difficult to break. For us, this may be true, but not for God. To Him, they are all the same.

He is working astonishing miracles with individuals hooked on hard drugs.

Not long ago, Pastor Ralph Wilkerson, of Melodyland Christian Center in Anaheim, California, told me a story showing how rapidly and effectively God can work on the most persistent addictions.

A clean-cut, clear-eyed young director of a TV program on which Ralph was a guest touched his coat sleeve, and said, "I have to talk with you for a minute."

"Sure."

"You may not recognize me, Pastor, but I was baptized in your baptistry. I was a mainliner!"

"You were?" It seemed unbelievable.

"Yes. Ten years ago, I came to Melodyland ministries, and I had—well, an almost unbelievable spiritual encounter. I used to think it was real excitement when I was high on drugs, but I never had anything that excited me more than an encounter with God. He changed my life, and I am serving the Lord today and enjoying my work in Christian TV beyond anything I've ever known.

"Pastor, what happened to me was incredible. I had a thirty-second recovery from the use of drugs!"

The young man who couldn't live without hard drugs ten years before hasn't touched them since.

While all recoveries from drug habits are not instant, many are, and many others respond over weeks, months, or as much as a year.

Both immediate and delayed miracle recoveries from drugs take place regularly at the Walter Hoving Home for troubled girls in Garrison, New York.

Here, the girls, disheartened by their inability to kick drug habits, try God, who accomplishes what they found to be impossible. Almost everyone has seen TRY GOD pendants and pins, produced under the trademark of Tiffany & Company, the prestigious chain of jewelry stores. Proceeds from sales of these pieces of jewelry are used by Walter Hoving, chairman of the board of Tiffany and a devout

Episcopalian, to support the home, which Hoving says is "run by the Lord."

Top-notch management has brought about a 94 percent record of recovery for those who stay for the required one year.

"More than nine out of ten girls who live in the home for a year, are free of drugs for three years or longer after leaving," says Hoving.

An average of cures in government and private secular institutions is 10 to 15 percent.

Hoving hastens to decline any credit. "It's not us," he insists. "We actually don't cure a heroin habit. We change girls through Christ."

The home accents a personal relationship with Jesus, upon whom the burden of changing individuals is placed.

Realizing that God loves them gives them support. They are not alone. New individuals in Christ, they are freed from what once appeared to be unyielding habits.

Graduates of the Hoving Home are grateful every time they see a TRY GOD pendant dangling around someone's neck. First, they know that funds raised from sales of this jewelry sustained them through their recovery year. Second, they realize that others like them are going to be reclaimed when they decide to take the high road, rather than the low road—when they decide to try God.

Perhaps the world's greatest Christian contribution to overcoming the drug habit is being made by David Wilkerson's Teen Challenge. Hundreds of thousands of hooked young people—and some not so young—have been liberated from drugs by Christ in more than eighty Teen Challenge Centers in the United States and more than one hundred centers elsewhere throughout the world. But Teen Challenge's influence ripples out from there. It is the model and inspiration for other Christian organizations formed for the same purpose.

Only a miracle from God saved and preserved the original Teen Challenge Center, when it was launched by David Wilkerson in a New York City ghetto.

David Wilkerson tells the thrilling story in his perennial best-seller, *The Cross and the Switchblade*. A member of the board at the start of Teen Challenge in 1960, I was present during the crisis of September, 1961, when a $15,000 certified check had to be paid to the second mortgage holders on the Teen Challenge building to prevent the organization from being thrown out into the street. One extension had already been given—September 1 to September 10. That date would be final!

Treasurer Paul DiLena reported to Pastor Wilkerson that the balance in Teen Challenge's bank account was fourteen dollars. Wilkerson asked God for a miracle and then told everybody in the center—drug addicts, gang members, and staff—that the center had been saved.

Cheering rocked the place.

"Let's go to the chapel and thank God!" he urged.

They did, praising the Lord for the money. Someone finally asked where Pastor Wilkerson had gotten the money.

David shook his head. He didn't have it yet, but it would be there for sure by September 10. He had just gotten the idea that they should all thank God in advance.

With this dynamic expression of faith, on September 8, Teen Challenge board members got on the phone, calling every likely prospect for the needed money. Results were nil. I accepted the task of calling Clement Stone, president of Combined Insurance Companies in Chicago—someone we had literally worn out with requests for help. I did it with no small amount of embarrassment, because Stone had been most generous. He had been filled in frequently on the center's progress—not just when his checks were needed.

I had to reinforce my backbone with prayer, because I

could visualize Clem Stone shuddering and hiding his checkbook when he learned who was calling.

Stone wasn't in, but his son came on the phone. I told him some of the human-interest stories: the heart-tugging recoveries from addictions and of apparently incorrigible, knife-wielding, thieving, sadistic gang members being completely and miraculously transferred into new creatures in Christ. I thanked him and his father for all they had done to support the center and help make possible a place where such wondrous things could happen.

The longer I talked, the harder it became to reach the point of the message. I either had to back off or blurt it out. I did the latter, bluntly asking for $15,000 within two days. I suggested that he not make a decision immediately but discuss the matter with his father.

"Please thank him for what he has already done. And then let's see what will happen."

With great relief, I hung up and prayed, thanked and praised God.

Nothing significant arrived in the mail on the ninth or tenth—only jingling small change.

During the mid-morning chapel service, David was interrupted by a rap at the door. A postman handed him a special-delivery letter, postmarked Chicago. Even as David opened it, he knew what was inside: a certified check from Clement Stone for $15,000.

A place where lost souls are found, Teen Challenge has been the model for lost-and-found organizations other than Hoving's home. One of them is the Fellowship Vine in Pasadena, California, the project of Nick Cadena, a "hopeless" heroin addict, who, for the last four years of his fifteen-year enslavement, stole five hundred thousand dollars to keep his one-hundred-dollar-a-day habit going.

Nick took every imaginable human measure to kick the habit, but agonizing desire always wrenched him back.

Only God could break him free, if someone would tell him how to find God.

A miracle happened at that point. He confided the problem to his pusher.

"That's easy," the fellow said. "There's a gal who occasionally holds miracle services at Angelus Temple: Kathryn Kuhlman."

So the pusher jeopardized the income from his best customer and drove him to the Angelus Temple. The music, the healing service, and the soothing spirit pervading the Temple brought a change and new hope to Nick Cadena. There he learned about Teen Challenge. As fast as he could, he visited Teen Challenge and submitted himself for healing.

"That's where I kicked the habit cold turkey, but not on my own," he admits. "It happened by the grace of God and the power of the Holy Spirit. It's now ten years since I've had drugs."

For a decade now, Cadena and his wife, Pauline, have dedicated their lives to bringing the cleansing and delivering power of Christ to other addicts. A part of their ministry is visiting inmates of prisons, county jails, and juvenile homes and preaching the Gospel of redemption to them.

Most of the residents of Fellowship Vine have been convicts, and almost all have been hooked on hard drugs.

"They kick the habit here," states Cadena. "Usually the crisis time is three days. They should hang in there for at least six months. Those who stay for a year will never revert."

Funded by donations, Fellowship Vine holds daily Bible lessons to help the born-again individuals mature spiritually. Residents attend a Christian church service each Sunday. Housework, yardwork, exercising, and reading occupy them. No outside jobs are permitted until they graduate. These positive-habit patterns for a year help keep them in a close relationship with Christ. This protects them after leaving the house.

A typical comment of residents who have been there for six months or more is, "I had doubts when I first came. Sometimes I thought I would split, but then I got this relationship with Christ. You don't just turn over a new leaf here. You get a new life from the Lord. Sure, I have some of the same problems that got me into drugs in the first place, but now I turn to God instead of drugs. Man, there's no comparison which is better."

To help graduates stay clear, ex-convicts organized a group called the Fellowship Men's Awakening, which meets periodically to hear Christian testimonies of others like themselves. Some grads give their own testimonies there and to church groups.

The theory is, if they're busy with the Lord, they will have less temptation to go back into drugs.

Although a small operation, Cadena's Fellowship Vine is important in two ways. It changes the lives of men; they come out different men than they came in. It is also an inspiration for imitation by other graduates of Teen Challenge, which continues to grow and offer new facilities and services.

The latest outgrowth of Teen Challenge is Christian Life Schools in various parts of the United States. Some sixty to seventy men are residents at any one time in a given Christian Life School. Each individual is expected to stay from eight to twelve months, to assure that his born-again experience and Christian habit patterns of turning to God rather than drugs will keep him in line permanently.

Glenn Timmons, director of the Riverside, California, Christian Life School, formerly an addict, offers impressive statistics on residents. A government-funded study of Teen Challenge by the National Institute of Drug Abuse shows that Teen Challenge's thirty-day rehabilitation program produces a 70 percent drug-recovery rate. The full eight-month to one-year course shows that 86 percent are drug free from five to seven years later.

These results, compared with those for psychological, sociological, and medical approaches of federal government hospitals, which result in 10 to 20 percent permanent recoveries, show convincingly that the Christian rebirth and resident habit-pattern training is from four to eight times more effective.

There is no reluctance on God's part to help anyone who invites Him to break a habit or addiction that is defiling and sabotaging the body or mind, for He wishes us to be pure.

> Know ye not that ye are the temple of God, and that the Spirit of God dwelleth in you? If any man defile the temple of God, him shall God destroy; for the temple of God is holy, which temple ye are.
>
> 1 Corinthians 3:16, 17

God's promises in the Bible tell us we needn't struggle alone with our problems, whether they are negative habits or something else. We are given this invitation in Psalms 55:22: "Cast thy burden upon the Lord, and he shall sustain thee . . . ."

Joy Dawson, of Youth With A Mission puts it this way: "I can't. *You* can and will, *now!*

6 Invisible Protectors

> ". . . If they found us, it would mean certain death . . . . We prayed to the Lord to blind their eyes to our home, asking that if they looked toward our home, they would see nothing but an empty field."

Strange, unpredictable things beyond our control happen to us all on occasion—things that threaten our well-being, safety, and even our lives: bizarre accidents, natural and man-made hazards, crimes of violence, dangers in various lines of work, and more.

When there seems to be no way out, there is always a way out through God, as promised in Psalms 46:1 "God is . . . a very present help in trouble."

That is exactly what innumerable individuals have found, including myself.

Some years ago, Paul Stutzman, a Detroit evangelist and I, his understudy, finished ministering in Memphis, and early the next morning, in a pelting rain, we started driving through the Great Smoky mountains, on our way to Lima, New York.

Paul was rejoicing over the wonderful deliverances we had seen at Faith Temple, by singing a little ditty which went, "The devil is mad, but I'm glad . . . ."

At that very moment, our right front wheel ran off the

road onto the rain-softened shoulder, the car flipped over, and we slid down the mountainside on the roof. As we struck the switchback road below, the car flipped again, landing on its wheels and catapulting the elderly man in the front seat to the road. His Bible flew in the air after him. The car began to turn over once more, about to crush the man in its path.

"God, help . . ." was all we could shout.

In that split second, the man saw the car ready to squash him and, with joyous calm, said to himself, "Hallelujah, this is it!"

Then in a flash, it seemed as if the hand of a mighty angel reversed the roll of the car and steadied it back on its wheels. The motor was still running, and we drove off under our own power, shaken up but unhurt, singing, "The devil is mad, and I'm glad . . . ."

Invisible protectors also gave a hand to Keith Winrich, vice president of the Evangelical Church Development Corporation.

As a teenager working on a farm, Keith attempted to jump on a giant, moving combine harvester machine, weighing many tons.

He slipped, and the next thing he knew, he was underneath.

"All I know is that it had to be in the providence of God that it happened, because of what happened."

If the machine had rolled over his head or the center of his body, it could have crushed his life out of him instantly.

Later, Keith learned, by comparing notes, that just prior to the time of the accident, God had spoken his name to a lady who was an intercessor. He told her to pray urgently, because Keith was in trouble. She called on God.

"As she did that, the machine was running over me," says Keith. "My feet flew up, caught on something underneath, pivoted my body, and kept the wheel from running across my heart or head. It came on my hip and across my rib cage and went off my shoulder—three inches from killing me.''

A doctor sped to the Winrich home. He took one look at Keith and shook his head solemnly.

''Don't wait for an ambulance,'' he urged. ''Rush him to the hospital in the car!''

There he was administered oxygen. Many doctors looked him over, finally putting him in the hands of a bone specialist. For the first four days, he was in such bad shape that they couldn't lay him out flat on the table for X rays. After that, they learned the extent of his injuries: five broken ribs, a broken collarbone, a punctured lung, by then filled with infection, and a smashed arm.

''If we can't clear up his infection, it will take his life,'' said the bone specialist.

It appeared they were going to operate on him immediately, to remove the infected lung, but the doctor in charge said, ''With an operation, you stand only a fifty-fifty chance to live. We'll watch it one more day.''

Prayers from Keith's Christian family, the woman who had originally been asked to pray, friends, and the Winrich's church congregation kept going almost continuously. And a camp meeting which Keith had planned to attend stopped for thirty minutes and three thousand people offered intercessory prayer for him.

The next morning he was prepared for surgery, and one more time they took X rays, letting him lie there while they developed them.

Suddenly the doctor came toward Keith, with the X rays of the previous day and the most recent ones in his hands.

''What's happened to you?'' he cried. ''You have a brand new lung in your body! Look at the difference!''

One X ray revealed a lung riddled with holes, and the

latest one showed a perfect lung. They took him off oxygen immediately.

The bone specialist on Keith's case said, "Every rib is knit perfectly."

He had not touched Keith's bones. Where the ribs had been broken in pieces and were puncturing the lung, the new X rays showed only a faint, hairline crack.

This had not been merely a physical healing. It had been a creative miracle from God. Despite his internal healing, Keith still had a totally paralyzed right arm and hand.

"The arm was completely paralyzed because the weight of the machine had crushed all the veins, arteries, and nerves of my shoulder," states Keith. "My arm swelled to twice its normal size. It was discolored and without feeling. You could hit it, and there was no sensation. They even talked of amputation."

Keith found subsequent events most exciting.

"Five days after the X rays showed I was healed, the doctor released me," he says. "I carried my arm home in a sling."

On a sunny morning, less than a week later, Keith woke from a sound sleep.

"I found both of my arms folded across my chest. I jerked my bad arm from under the sheet. All the swelling and discoloration were gone, and all the feeling returned. It was as if nothing had ever happened to me."

No one need convince Sweden-born Bengt Junvik that prayer can work miracles.

About to attend an annual meeting of an aviation mission in Alaska, he was asked to deliver a new Cessna aircraft for a flying service.

After arrival in Kenai, he was held up by storms on the final leg of his flight. On Wednesday morning, May 3, 1972, he was told there would be a slight break in the weather and that the route through Rainy Pass toward McGrath would be open.

So he filed his flight plan, remembering that the law of Alaska made it mandatory to carry supplies. For the short flight he took several strips of beef jerky, some crackers, hard candy, several pieces of chocolate, and three small cans of water. He was kidded about the water, because there was still plenty of snow in the mountains.

A friend tossed in a sleeping bag for him, and he took off. It seemed a routine flight, even though visibility decreased and he was confronted with a choice of which of two valleys to follow.

The ceiling began to lower even more, and then something unexpected happened. He had been following a riverbed and, as he checked below, he saw the ground quickly rising.

It was no big deal. He would just turn around and head back.

The weather continued to deteriorate. He started his turn to get out of there, when high-velocity winds, called mountain waves, spilled over peaks into the canyon, creating powerful downdrafts that made the Cessna sink rapidly.

"I gave the bird full power, changed my direction, heading into the wind, fully expecting to pick up lift and start climbing out of there, but I was still going down."

A rocky ridge suddenly appeared before him. He figured on heading for the lowest spot, but didn't quite make it, crunching right into a pile of rocks and flipping upside-down.

"It was kind of a shocking experience," he explains. "I hadn't experienced a bump, didn't have a scratch. Automatically I ripped my safety belt open and fell down, grabbing for the door handle to jump out, because I figured the aircraft would catch fire, but it didn't happen."

There was nothing inviting outside, so he just lay quietly, asking, "Lord, why in the world did this happen to me?"

The moment he said it, he knew he was there to stay for a while. Clouds were closing in so fast that he couldn't even see the wingtip. He figured it was a miracle that the aircraft had been set down so gently in its upside-down position and that nothing seemed to be damaged. Not even a window had been broken, assuring that he could be reasonably comfortable. Wind whistled around him, and he noted with thankfulness that if the aircraft had been right-side up, it would have been lifted by gusts and battered to pieces on the rocks.

All he could see from the windows were giant boulders and snowdrifts building higher as swirling snow sifted down.

Why hadn't he taken more food? Previously he had always prepared well for any eventualities. It was understandable that he hadn't installed a portable transmitter—a locator beacon—because he was only ferrying an aircraft which didn't belong to him, but there was no excuse for not having borrowed one for the trip.

"It was a humbling experience to be so utterly helpless," he says. "I knew the Lord had a purpose, but it was still hard to understand why I was in this situation without even a scratch if I was going to spend the rest of my days there."

The first night went by, and it wasn't unbearably cold in the sleeping bag. Bengt Junvik's major concern was that his family would have to get the shocking message that he was overdue. He prayed that his family would have faith that he was all right.

Shortly after landing, he had started to keep a diary, making a calendar and winding his watch at a certain time each day, so he wouldn't lose track of time. All the while, snow continued to fall.

Although empty inside, he rationed a little of his limited supply of food for each day. For the first four days, he didn't leave the airplane, lying still so that he wouldn't burn up energy and require more food.

Then he noted a marked change in the altimeter, which works like a barometer—a change in the weather. Great!

Now that fair conditions were on the way, a search could be started for him.

Only on that evening, Saturday, did he step outside, seeing mountains on three sides—an opening only on the side where he had entered.

"I had a new appreciation of the miracle that I had been a part of," he says.

All three cans of water were already gone, but he could now eat snow. Certainly with clearing weather, the Air Force's Search and Rescue Team and the Civil Air Patrol would be out to find him.

"But nobody showed up that evening," he relates.

Maybe it hadn't cleared up yet in Anchorage.

"That night I shall always remember, because it was an experience that stands out in my mind so vividly—the total awareness that God was in the process of doing something positive. It was so exciting, there was no way I could sleep.

"All I could see was thousands of people praying for me—a fantastic experience. The reality of God's presence at a time like that is overwhelming."

Early next morning, he saw a world of dazzling whiteness around him. The wind had swept the aircraft's wing clean, and the tranquility of the scene was majestic, overpowering.

That afternoon, he walked out on the wing, hoping to see a rescue aircraft. Then he heard it—the motor of an airplane—and saw a C–130 coming over the horizon.

Wearing a bright yellow sweater and jumping on the wing, he used a small mirror to reflect the sunlight.

His heart sank!

The C–130 just kept going. Then he realized the problem. In his peculiar position, no aircraft could spot him as it approached. This could only be done for a fleeting second as it passed directly overhead.

Here was a perfect day, made by God for a rescue, and the searcher had missed him.

In this long, long period alone, when all there was to do was think, Bengt Junvik gained a new perspective on life and values.

"I found a new awareness of the preciousness of time," he explains, "and said to the Lord, 'If You ever get me out of here, don't let me forget that time is not my own, but a gift from You.' "

Junvik's main concern was not for dying. He felt it is not how long we live that's important, but what we do with our lives. It bothered him to have been a cause for agony to his wife and family.

"I tried awfully hard to convince God that my family needed me for a while. It's a humbling experience to realize that maybe nobody needs you."

Now it was the middle of the next week, and he had a silent assurance that God was well aware of his circumstances, and that He could be trusted.

"I felt I was on the winning side again when I committed myself to God."

By the second weekend, he had high hopes once more, but the weekend came and went, and there was no sign of rescue.

On Monday morning, May 15—the thirteenth day—he had eaten his last piece of beef jerky, and things looked grim.

Again clouds had come over, but that noon it started to clear again. Then it hit him hard.

" 'This is for real. I'm not going to be rescued.' I felt depressed, but wonderful things happen when you run out of options. I said, 'Lord, I'm willing to face whatever You have for me, but please take care of my family and give them peace and strength.' "

Once more the peace came back, and his prayer changed to a conversation with God.

"Lord, I know You're trying to teach me patience, but I think I've got the idea now. I know it will take a miracle, and I don't know how You're going to do it, but. . . ."

Suddenly he heard a miracle overhead—a helicopter. He jumped out of his sleeping bag and ran out on the wing, waving his hands wildly. He kept running.

His heart almost stopped, because the helicopter continued going on. Then, joy of joys, it circled and headed back.

They *had* seen him!

Never before had the noise of an engine sounded so beautiful.

Junvik gestured toward a flat place for the chopper to land. The pilot spotted it and landed.

"Praise the Lord for guys like you," shouted Junvik to him.

"If you think *you're* happy, what do you think we are? We just started looking for you this noon." Then the pilot laughed. "It was funny," he said to Junvik. "When you thought I'd missed you, you started running so fast, I thought you were trying to catch me."

Bengt Junvik knew some people would call his rescue luck, but he knew that prayer had done it.

When Junvik was reunited with his family in Anchorage, he found that a businessman friend was with them. This man had organized the search and kept it going day after day, despite discouragements.

A number of times searchers had been ready to give up, but prayer power had kept up his determination. As he admitted to Junvik, "I only did what the Lord told me to do."

And now for a real cliff-hanger!

It all began when Joe Stupak, of San Pedro, California, was a teenager who didn't know God at all. He suspected that there was a Higher Power but had to find out for sure. He looked into Eastern religions and into numerous Western philosophers, but none of them had real answers. They didn't know who God was, nor could they prove His existence. The sermons he heard created more doubt than faith.

"Maybe God kept me from finding Him there for a specific purpose," he says. "Finally, in desperation, I cried, 'God whatever You are, wherever You are, I can't find You.' "

A short time later, God gave Joe an awesome demonstration, not only that He exists, but that He cares for Joe personally.

Always involved in scientific projects, Joe, who was later to design a robot for the space shuttle, needed a certain type of motor, and he knew exactly where he could find it . . . in one of the fighter aircraft which had crashed in the mountains of Orange County, behind El Toro Naval Air Station.

Well into a cloudy afternoon, Joe and his brothers started the steep climb. High on a ridge, they decided to go in opposite directions. Farther and farther Joe climbed, spotting a number of aircraft but stopping at none of them. It was almost as if he were driven.

Something odd is going on that I don't understand, he said to himself.

Suddenly it was dark.

Because of the overcast, he hadn't noticed the sun go down.

Now he was frightened.

He was dressed only in jeans and a T-shirt, hardly the clothing for a night in the mountains. He came onto a dry, winding riverbed and decided to follow it. The darkness was so impenetrable that he could see nothing but the reflection of sand in front of him.

Then, all of a sudden, the sand stopped. He felt ahead to find what was there.

"I reached with my foot and then with my hand. There seemed to be a sheer drop off. I went to the left and felt a sheer cliff. On the right, there seemed to be some bushes, so I pushed into those bushes and started to fall. I reached down and grabbed what appeared to be a tree and climbed back up to the ledge."

Now he began to wonder, "What's going to become of me? I can't stay here. If this rain gets any harder, a flash flood might develop."

He began to fear being washed off a cliff and smashed to death on the rocks below. He knew he had to get out of there. And at that instant he became aware of a voice speaking—not a voice outside himself. It was like something echoing through his mind, sounding very clear and calm. There was no question what the words were. He thought he wasn't hearing what he was hearing but was just very tired.

"Should I climb down the tree?" Joe asked.

And the answer was, "No, it's fifty feet down."

That seemed reasonable to Joe. After all, he had climbed back on the ledge from it.

"What can I do? Can I go down the ledge in front?" he asked.

The answer was, "It's only about ten feet down. You may hurt yourself some, but you may be able to get out."

Joe rejected that as a ridiculous idea. Nobody in his right mind would risk jumping in the blackness without being certain how far down it was.

"Well," he asked himself. "What's left?"

At that instant, he began to realize that something very special was happening to him. He was carrying on a most unusual communication.

"What do I do now?" Joe asked the voice.

"Climb the cliff."

Joe replied, "Whatever you are, if I climb the cliff, when will I get off?"

The voice responded, "*You* pick the time!"

"Well," Joe said to himself, "I'll play this silly game. Let's make it ten o'clock!" And he started up the cliff in the pitch dark. It actually wasn't too difficult, for some unknown reason.

"It seemed every time I would put a hand on a rock it would come free. Every time I reached out and grabbed something which gave me support, it was alive: a tree, a plant, or some desert grass growing in the crevices of the rock."

After a while the terrain seemed to level off quite a bit, and Joe could get up on his knees. He didn't know exactly how long he had been climbing. Then he heard some sounds.

It was a search party!

Joe and they called back and forth, and soon a light came on, but not in the place where Joe was expecting it. The light was from below. He realized his sense of direction was off, due to disorientation.

Then a second light came on against the cliff, and mountain rangers began to climb up. They finally reached him.

As they cautiously went back down, Joe could see the whole area. He had climbed a cliff several thousand feet—it was actually an overhang—to the one and only position in which the rescue party could have seen him. Joe and the party passed the tree he had been in. In the lights, Joe checked the drop. It was indeed about fifty feet down! They passed the little ledge. It was ten feet down, as had been told to him.

"As we walked into a circle, there was a big fire, and I found myself next to a man," says Joe. "What time is it?" Joe asked.

"Well, it's ten o'clock!"

"*Exactly*, what time is it?" Joe insisted. "I want to know exactly!"

"It's funny you should ask that," the man replied. "I'm

the chief ranger, and just before we got a call to come up here, I checked my watch with the wall clock. But for some reason, I wasn't certain it was right, so I called the time service, and I know to within one second it is exactly ten o'clock.''

Joe thought about it and finally concluded, ''There was no way, no other explanation I could find, but that God Himself had set that up. He knew that I needed that sort of thing as proof. . . . There was no other power that could have done this, and then I knew that God had created heaven and earth, and that He really cared about me.''

God's demonstrations of His power to protect are particularly comforting in this age of violence, when conscienceless brutality, rape, and murder are commonplace.

Not long ago, Howard Conatser told the story which opens this book and the following one to a national TV audience.

One evening an attractive young lady stopped at a 7–Eleven store to pick up a few items. She had not locked her car, and when she returned, a man rose up from the floor behind her. He commanded her to drive off to a lonely place, where she knew her cries for help would not be heard.

Frightened, she blurted, ''Who are *you?*''

''No matter. Get going!''

She turned and faced him, ''You can't touch me. I'm a child of God!''

For an instant, he glared wildly at her, then he scrambled out of the car and ran as fast as he could.

Said Conatser, ''I believe that man recognized that she lived in the Kingdom and had the protection of the Kingdom power of God and His angels.''

No matter where danger exists, God is there, ready for us to call upon Him.

A Methodist missionary in Zaire, Africa, Reverend Harold Amstatz and his wife Elsie lived right in the path of one of the most brutal bloodbaths in the history of Africa.

During the invasion of Zaire from Angola, when rebels started with the first house in an area and slaughtered whites and blacks in every house, Pastor and Mrs. Amstatz saw the tidal wave of terror sweep toward them.

Rebels with guns ran up and down the streets, yelling "Missionaire, missionaire!"

Reverend Amstatz reports, "We knew if they found us, it would mean certain death."

Things happened so fast that there was no human way for them to hide. All the telltale signs were there to invite in the killers: the house itself, an antenna in the backyard, a car in a carport in front of the house, and a Methodist mission card in the window.

As the rebels entered houses methodically, shooting or butchering occupants, Pastor Amstatz began to repeat the Ninety-first Psalm:

> He that dwelleth in the secret place of the most High shall abide under the shadow of the Almighty. I will say of the Lord, He is my refuge and my fortress: my God; in him will I trust. Surely he shall deliver thee from the snare of the fowler, and from the noisome pestilence. He shall cover thee with his feathers, and under his wings shalt thou trust: his truth shall be thy shield and buckler. Thou shalt not be afraid for the terror by night; nor for the arrow that flieth by day; Nor for the pestilence that walketh in darkness; nor for the destruction that wasteth at noonday. A thousand shall fall at thy side, and ten thousand at thy right hand; but it shall not come nigh thee. Only with thine eyes shalt thou behold and see the reward of the wicked. Because thou hast made the Lord, which is my refuge, even the most High, thy habitation; There shall no evil befall thee, neither shall any plague come nigh thy dwelling. For

he shall give his angels charge over thee, to keep thee in all thy ways. They shall bear thee up in their hands, lest thou dash thy foot against a stone.

The rebels closed in, shots ringing through the streets. Pastor Amstatz held fast to the words "A thousand shall fall at thy side, and ten thousand at thy right hand; but it shall not come nigh thee."

He says, "We prayed to the Lord to blind their eyes to our home, asking that if they looked toward our home, they would see nothing but an empty field."

For eight days, the reign of terror continued, but the rebels walked, ran, or drove their vehicles by the Amstatz home, as if it weren't there. So far as they were concerned, it wasn't. God's promise in the Ninety-first Psalm saw to that.

For many of us, threatening situations requiring a miracle usually develop by accident, negligence, or poor planning—occasionally all three. But some also come about because certain individuals deliberately take part in high-risk activities.

One of these risks is smuggling Bibles into Iron Curtain countries, particularly the Soviet Union. For twenty-five years, George Derkatch, of World Christian Ministries, in Toronto, Canada, has coordinated such an undertaking, even, on occasion, personally delivering Bibles to the estimated 30 to 50 million above-ground or under-ground Christians in the USSR.

"The Bible in the Russian language is the most powerful weapon to destroy the works of the enemy," he explains. "The law of the Bible says we should go into all the world and preach the Gospel."

An appalling shortage of Bibles exists there, so dedicated individuals brave the dangers, with only the protection of God to save them from being caught and imprisoned.

Derkatch tells how God took care of a Russian border guard: "A few years ago, I was taking in two hundred Bibles in the trunk of a small Renault car. When I was nearing the border, I saw the sign, YOU ARE NOW APPROACHING THE FORBIDDEN AREA. BE SURE YOUR DOCUMENTS ARE IN ORDER.

"The minute I saw that sign, the faith and boldness that I had left me, and I said to my friend, 'I'm scared.'

"Then I prayed and said, 'Lord, this is not a joke. I'm not here because I want to be here. I'm here because You have called me to this work, and those brethren, my brethren, need the Bible.'

"So I prayed desperately before God. And then, all of a sudden I felt the power and presence of God coming into the car, and I told my friend, who had been driving, to move to the other side of the car and let me drive."

Derkatch got behind the wheel. It was eleven kilometers from the border, eight miles or less, and it was as if the car were transported several times faster than it could normally travel, arriving in a few minutes.

Derkatch felt he was no longer in charge of his conduct or words. It seemed to him a Higher Power was in command.

"I jumped out of the car and said, 'Good evening, sir. I've been here before. You have a great country.'

"The border guard said, 'Show me your passport.' "

Derkatch did.

"What do you have in your trunk?"

Derkatch invited him to look. How can one hide four cartons containing two hundred Russian Bibles in a trunk as small as that of a Renault?

The guard looked intently. He would have had to be blind not to see the cartons of Bibles. Perhaps he was, for an instant, because he said, "Close the trunk."

He took Derkatch's passport, stamped it, and opened the gate, and Derkatch, his friend, and the Bibles were in.

Derkatch tells of another miraculous delivery of Bibles

into the Soviet Union, showing that God also performs miracles with a humorous twist.

A Christian man and his wife from the Soviet Union visited him in his Toronto offices. When they saw the large number of Russian Bibles and songbooks available, the woman knelt down and said, "Dear God, there are more Bibles and songbooks here than we have in the entire nation."

The man remarked, "I would like to take five hundred Bibles and songbooks to distribute back home."

"Fine," replied Derkatch. "I will be glad to give them to you, but how will you get them across?"

"I don't know, but God tells me I should take them."

Derkatch had them packed in five cartons and labeled with the couple's name and address. They took the cartons with them. When they reached the Soviet customs and the cartons rested on a counter to be inspected, they prayed that the Bibles would get through, no matter if it meant imprisonment or death to them.

At that point, the man became critically ill, grew pale, and passed out in a heap. In the midst of the confusion, he was rushed to a hospital.

Three days later, he and his wife, who had remained at his bedside, returned to their apartment, where they were almost floored with amazement. On the floor of their bedroom were the five cartons, which had not even been opened.

Customs, which should have prevented the Bibles and songbooks from coming in, had actually delivered them to their destination.

No matter what the impending danger, God has a miracle to handle it.

In his book, *Death of a Guru,* Rabindranath R. Maharaj describes a miraculous deliverance.

While a collegian vacationing at his aunt's cocoa plantation in the jungle highlands of India, he was admiring the glories of the natural setting, with his back to a sheer cliff, when he was surprised by a large, thick-bodied snake with a hooded head. The first thought that hit him was *cobra!* Its look of evil almost overwhelmed Rabindranath.

Now it was near enough to touch. Almost paralyzed with fear, he knew he could not risk stepping backwards another six inches, toward the cliff's edge.

Just as the snake reared its head to strike, he remembered his mother's words that if he were ever in extreme danger, he should call on the name of Jesus.

"Jesus, help me!" he tried to yell, but the desperate cry stopped short of sound.

"To my utter astonishment, the snake dropped its head to the ground, turned clumsily around, and wriggled off at a great rate into the underbrush . . . ."

Although it is wise to exercise every precaution and careful planning wherever danger threatens, we know that when our own defenses fail us, we have access to God's.

7 Little Miracles and a Great God

> "... a dust devil—a tiny whirlwind—moved down the road toward them. The driver . . . and . . . his passengers, watched in fascination . . . ."

Is God too big and busy to be involved in the minutia of our lives?

In His mightiness and vastness, God seems too great to be aware of, let alone concerned with, the details of our lives. But the very fact that He is involved is proof of His greatness.

I used to wonder, *With four billion other people to look after, how can He possibly find time for little me?*

And then I came across the description of God in Isaiah 57:15: ". . . the high and lofty One that inhabiteth eternity . . . ."

It is not a question of how He can find time, because God inhabits eternity and is, therefore, beyond the limitations of time.

C. S. Lewis has given us a good illustration in *Mere Christianity*. An author is penning the words: "There was a knock at the door.

" 'Who is it?' he asked."

In that moment, the phone rang, and it was an emergency call to Timbuktu. On his return, a year later, he sits down to pick up the story where he left off.

"Now where was I?" he asked. "Oh, yes, there was a knock at the door."

" 'Who is it?' he asked.

" 'It is I,' came the reply."

Between the question and answer in the life of the characters there is one split second. In the life of the author, an entire year.

In other words, the author is beyond the time limitation of his characters.

God not only has all eternity for each one of us; it is as if you are the only person in the entire universe.

Despite the fact that God inhabits eternity, we hesitate to bother Him with our problems that fall short of catastrophic, important though they are to us. Yet His own words tell us that His eye is on the sparrow.

His tender and loving watchfulness over us is clearly shown through two incidents in the life of Carolyn Scheer, a member of the Pasadena, California, chapter of Women's Aglow Fellowship, a Christian organization.

Carolyn owns a one-hundred-year-old, intricately engraved pocket watch, which she inherited from her mother, who, in turn, had inherited it from her mother. An expert on watches appraised its value at more than one thousand dollars.

One Sunday morning, Carolyn and her husband, my coauthor James F. Scheer, were about to attend church services with Ray Carlson, president of International Films, a Christian motion-picture firm, and his wife Joy.

Carolyn couldn't find her watch. Earlier in the week, she had left home in a hurry and, instead of attaching the watch to her dress, had put it into the side pocket of her purse. She remembered leaving her purse unguarded on one occasion.

Now she inserted her hand into the side pocket.

She found nothing there!

She became so nervous that Jim joined the search. They methodically went through every purse and jewelry case in the master bedroom and bathroom. Then they looked under the queen-size bed, under chairs, and under cushions of chairs. Finally, they took all the bedding off the bed, without finding the watch.

Carolyn, in frustration, said, "I don't know if I can even go to church with the watch on my mind."

"You shouldn't let that stop you," replied Jim. "God is first—far more important than your watch. Let's go to church anyway!"

This made sense to Carolyn.

Together, they made up the bed, smoothed the white bedspread, straightened the room, surveyed every flat surface, in a final search for the watch, went downstairs, locked the townhouse securely, and left for the church service.

After brunching with the Carlsons, they stopped at their home to talk, but Carolyn soon became restless, finally telling her hosts what was troubling her.

"Carolyn, you know nothing is lost to the Lord," Joy reassured her. "All we need to do is reaffirm our belief and faith in Jesus, and you will get your watch back."

Joy and Ray led the prayer. Then Carolyn and Jim left them to renew the search.

What happened after they unlocked and entered their townhouse raised goose bumps on their arms and gave them an eerie feeling.

Everything seemed exactly as they had left it.

Carolyn went upstairs to change her clothes. Jim was still downstairs. Suddenly he heard Carolyn scream and call, "Jim, come quickly!"

He did.

"Look!" she cried out, pointing to the white bedspread.

There in the very center of the bed was the antique, gold watch.

Another incident made Carolyn and Jim aware once more how the Lord works miracles, if we invite Him into our hearts and daily activities.

Carolyn had been experiencing depleted energy and recurring depression. In the depth of her blues, she found her faith wavering and began to wonder if she had been forgotten even by God.

On one of her more cheerful days, she was asked to pose for a color photograph to be used in *Testimony* magazine in connection with a condensation of the book *Tell It On the Mountain,* the autobiography of William R. Lasky, which Jim had coauthored.

Several months later, the article was published. It included Carolyn's photo and a lengthy caption, mentioning her membership in the Pasadena chapter of Aglow. Soon after that, a letter came to her from a person she did not know—Jane Lauer, of Columbus, Ohio. It had been sent to her in care of *Testimony* magazine.

Mrs. Lauer had seen her photo in the publication and was prompted to write her. Following are pertinent parts of her letter:

Dear Sister in Christ,

We are not only sisters in the Lord, but Aglow sisters as well. I am writing you because I felt the Lord was telling me to. The first of January this year, we came to California.

I did not write or call, using all kinds of excuses, such as, I am not sure! *Why,* God? and all the other standard questions that go through one's mind. Also I do not have your home address, but feel if God has some reason—whatever it is—the address I am using will enable me to reach you.

I must ask you and my Lord to forgive me for waiting so long, but you still keep coming into my mind, so here goes.

I feel for some reason God would have me tell you how

much He loves you and He wants to encourage you over
and over again . . . .

Out of obedience to Him,
Love in Christ,
Jane Lauer

Two thrilling miracles—a mini miracle wrapped in a
major one—have left Patricia Martin overwhelmed with
God's love and Fatherly concern over every detail in our
lives.

Writing in *Testimony,* she revealed the details of her
unique experience.

After teaching school all day in Glendale, Oregon, Patricia would return to her rented home, cook for her young
sons, Paul and William, and a niece living with them, and
then play sacred songs on her treasured violin.

On a Friday night in winter, she felt a strong urge to take
her sons and niece on an overnight trip to Grants Pass.
Earlier she had washed some clothes, and it appeared to her
that the hot-water heater wasn't working quite right, but
she gave it only a passing thought.

Patricia found herself hurriedly packing. She wondered
why the big rush. After locking up, she told two neighbors
where they were going.

Near Wolf Creek, halfway toward their destination, the
boys became restless and irritable, finally getting on Patricia's nerves. She suggested having dinner and then turning back. Instantly a voice within her said, "No. Go ahead
and have some fun. You work so hard. You need this out-
ing."

The meal settled the boys down, so the Martin party
continued to Grants Pass, where they checked in at the
Uptown Motel and went to bed.

Around eight o'clock on Saturday morning, a sharp
knock at the door startled Patricia from a sound sleep. She

was surprised to see a policeman standing outside.

"Are you Mrs. Martin?" he asked.

Patricia nodded.

"Your landlady described your car. That's how we tracked you down," he explained. "Disaster at home! Phone your landlady right away!"

Trembling, Patricia did.

Her landlady's voice burst through the receiver: "The hot-water heater exploded! The house blew up. The roof's off and walls are down! Neighbors are cleaning up the debris. Better come right back!"

Patricia almost cried in gratitude.

God had gotten them out of the house to save their lives!

She, the boys, and her niece knelt to thank and praise the Lord.

When they reached Glendale and rounded the last corner, they saw the wreckage that had been their house. Neighbors explained that the water heater, located in the attic, above the head of Patricia's bed, had exploded with such force that it broke windows on the whole block and was heard for three miles. Part of the heater had blasted through the ceiling above Patricia's bed, and the rest had rocketed through the roof and buried itself in the ground, a block away.

Patricia assured herself that their possessions could be replaced by insurance. Then, all at once, she remembered something—her most-valued treasure: the violin.

It had probably been shattered to matchsticks.

In any event, she asked a neighbor about it.

All he knew was that the violin case had been hurled outside, like almost everything else in the house, and that someone had brought the case to a nearby hardware store for safekeeping.

Patricia hurried over to the store with many neighbors,

who were as curious as she was to see what had happened.

"I found the case there without a scratch," she said. "I opened it and discovered the violin in flawless condition."

She started to play. To her utter amazement, the violin was in perfect tune!

While in Rhodesia during a period of bloodshed, Pastor Kent Tucker, of Lake Avenue Congregational Church, in Pasadena, California, met a Christian who had just experienced a thrilling miracle.

This man was driving three non-Christians down a dirt, country road when he felt an overpowering compulsion to pray.

Why pray? For whom? For what?

But the intense urge continued, even more powerfully, so he said to his passengers, "I feel a strong compulsion to pull over and pray."

They patronized him with looks that said, "Well, if you must. . . ," or "We wouldn't want you to drive with your eyes closed."

So he stopped.

While he was praying, a dust devil—a tiny whirlwind—moved down the road toward them.

The driver opened his eyes and, with his passengers, watched in fascination. They all gasped when they saw what it uncovered in the road ten feet ahead of the car—a giant land mine!

Occasionally a mini miracle from God shows a definite sense of humor.

Pat Robertson tells about a Christian in India who was experiencing lean days financially and prayed for some good food.

As an act of faith, he placed a frying pan on the fire,

whose smoke went out through a hole in his humble dwelling's roof.

Something distracted him for an instant, and when he turned back, he saw a large fish flip-flopping in the hot frying pan.

As he looked upward to praise the Lord, he saw a giant pelican perched above the hole, ruefully glancing down at the one that got away.

8 Money Miracles

"What am I supposed to do when I get to Denver?" he kept asking himself. "See the same people and get the same old rejections?" But he obeyed instructions.

If anybody needed a King-sized miracle, Pat Boone did. That was in the late 1960s, when I was introduced to him by George Otis, a Christian business executive and consultant, and spent an afternoon and evening praying with him on the crest of the Hollywood Hills, overlooking Hollywood, Los Angeles, Beverly Hills, and the San Fernando Valley.

Our meeting is described in the first chapter of Pat's best-seller, *A New Song*.

Pat was in trouble financially. He hadn't had a hit record in a long time, and his marriage was teetering dangerously on a cliff's edge. His greatest financial millstone was the Oakland Oaks, his professional basketball team, operating in the red and greedily swallowing every cent of his declining income from other sources.

As we prayed, Pat rededicated himself to God. A new man came down from the mountain.

A short time later, I gave a talk on the gift of faith at the home of George Otis, and some forty individuals attended, including Pat, looking pale and drawn, and

Shirley Boone, who sat in the rear.

Pat needed $2 million the next day to keep from going bankrupt, and he confessed to me: "Harald I didn't want to come tonight or see anyone. I have just been informed by my attorney and business manager that I am bankrupt. Why prolong the agony, because it is inevitable? They insist I declare bankruptcy tomorrow."

"Pat, God isn't going to let you go bankrupt. God's reputation is at stake in your life. Before, it wasn't, but now, if you go bankrupt, everyone is going to say, 'Sure, Pat turned to the Lord when he was on the ropes. This was his escape.' "

Pat, George Otis, Harald McNaughton, a dynamic Christian businessman, and I were standing near the swimming pool, when I reminded Pat of my talk on faith. He was not receptive. "It works for you, Harald, but not for me."

At that point, George Otis said, "Let's lay hands on him."

We did and George prayed, "Lord, give Pat a massive, immediate miracle."

Not many hours later, a total stranger appeared from Washington, D.C. and bought the Oakland Oaks team from Pat for $2 million. Positive overtones of the miracle spread to every phase of his life.

There's an amusing sequel to the Oakland Oaks story.

While I was staying at the Omni Hotel in Norfolk, Virginia, I had dinner with Leonard Strelitz, chairman of the United Jewish Appeal, who asked me how well I knew Pat Boone.

"Very well," I told im. "Why do you ask?"

"Do you think he would be willing to host the Israeli ambassador so that we could invite in influential and wealthy Jewish men for the ambassador to talk to about money for Israel?"

"I think so, but I'll have to discuss it with him."

This whole trend of events made me see an opportunity to show Strelitz the dimension of miracles in the life of Christians, so I said that the book, *A New Song,* would tell him something about Pat's and my relationship. My assistant, Dana Pereau, went upstairs for the book, and I read excerpts to Strelitz. When I came to the miracle part about the Oakland Oaks, he almost yelled, "Don't tell me who bought the Oakland Oaks for $2 million from him. I'll tell you who. It was Earl Forman."

"How did you know?" I asked.

"Because I bought the Oakland Oaks from him for $2 million, and will you pray to God that He will send someone to buy the team from me for $2 million?"

It seems that I often meet individuals when they require a financial miracle.

The first time I heard David Wilkerson, he was speaking to a group of ministers in Brooklyn. His struggling ministry was deep in the red and had to terminate its contract to broadcast over station WOR.

This struck me as sad, because David's program was a great Christian witness to the world. Individuals who had been miraculously cured of addiction to narcotics, in the days when a heroin addiction was considered absolutely hopeless, gave their testimonies on this program and encouraged other addicts to be delivered of their habits through Christ.

When David announced, "We are four thousand dollars in the red, and today I must sever the contract with WOR," I found myself asking from the audience, "If you had five thousand dollars, would it make any difference?"

"It would make all the difference in the world!"

He looked at me as if I had the $5,000.

I didn't have the money, but one thing had been impressed upon me: We never have to ask, How much money do we need? But, Does God want a job done? If He wants it

done, we can go ahead and know the money will be
there.

An idea came to my mind, and David and I went to see a
prominent Christian editor and described the financial problem. Then I said, "Please, I believe God can tell you where
there is ten thousand dollars." My faith had gone up by
now. And he replied, "Yes, I believe I know where.
There's a man in town who happens to have two hundred
million dollars in his foundation."

"Who's that?"

"Clement Stone."

"Will you write us a letter of introduction?"

He did.

We told Clement Stone the whole story, and then I said:
"What is ten thousand dollars compared to your vast resources?" It was an inspired compliment, because he came
through. It was like the inspired compliment God wishes us
to give Him: "Lord, I've got this need, but what is it compared with Your infinite resources? You own the cattle on a
thousand hills."

We must see our needs, our tiny needs, in relation to the
greatness of His supply. The destroyer of faith is seeing the
greatness of our need filling our whole horizon. We've got
to view it in the proper relationship to God's unlimited supply.

Some of the most beautiful financial miracles come about
without the persons involved announcing to anyone that
they have a need.

Such miracles of supply are daily affairs at L'Abri,
world-famous retreat for prayer, Bible studies, Christian
talks, and fellowship, in Switzerland.

Run by Francis and Edith Schaeffer and their family,
L'Abri has no visible means of support. Yet it flourishes
year after year on invisible support: prayer and faith.

One of the most fascinating miracles to come out of L'Abri is that concerning Jane Stuart Smith.

An opera singer of considerable stature, Jane was moved by the power of God to quit her career at its peak, to give up using her glorious voice to sing with one-hundred-piece orchestras in celebrated opera houses throughout the world. She turned her back on applause, fame, and rich financial reward and joined the staff of L'Abri to serve God full time.

Her only tie to the past was an extensive wardrobe of museum-piece costumes. One of them, for a role in *Turandot,* had a train that extended almost from one end of the stage to the other. All of them had been custom-tailored to her precise body measurements for many and varied roles in different operas.

One morning, as she made beds and fed the chickens, she realized she had not given her life completely to God, because she still had costumes that tied her to the past.

L'Abri desperately needed a chapel, and Jane pledged to give her costumes to the Lord for this project.

As Edith Schaeffer put it at the time, "That was a very romantic idea—lovely, but, as far as common sense goes, what were we going to do with the costumes? How could they build the chapel?"

Both Jane and Edith prayed for a way to translate the costumes into money.

Prayers continued for two years, and nothing happened. Suddenly a telegram arrived one morning for Jane. It was from a Yugoslavian opera singer, who asked if she could meet Jane in Milan, Italy, to look at the costumes.

To be acceptable they would have to be for the roles that she sang and fit exactly: size, height, waistline. Even gloves, shoes, and hairpieces had to fit properly.

The two met in the large apartment of a friend of Jane's, where Jane spread out every garment, covering most of the floor.

The Yugoslavian singer was flabbergasted, says Edith.
"They're *all* the costumes I need. I sing all these parts.
Fantastic!"

But would they fit?

She tried them on, and each one conformed to her body
as if it had been custom-designed to fit her. In excitement
she bought the entire wardrobe.

So Jane's costumes became the start of the walls of
L'Abri chapel.

A complex miracle such as Jane Stuart Smith's was the
farthest thing from the mind of William Converse Jones, of
Pasadena, California. All he wanted was a small, simple
straightforward miracle.

One of the top producers in the San Marino offices of
Coldwell Banker, a prominent real estate company, Bill,
some years ago, while he was in the public-relations and
advertising business, needed a six-hundred-dollar miracle.
He had been more liberal than he had realized with auto-
graphs on the bottom of checks and had overdrawn his
checking account by six hundred dollars.

Zealous to keep his credit record good, Bill knew that,
before midnight, he would have to mail the bank a check to
cover the overdraft.

Surely before he closed his office at 5:30 P.M., he would
somehow receive the needed money! All day long, he tried
to collect bad debts and solicit new accounts, in hope of
getting an advance on services, but, despite his best efforts,
nothing good happened. Now it was 5:30.

Unhappy, Bill told himself, "Well, God has let me
down."

When he reached Lake Avenue Congregational Church
in Pasadena for a dinner board meeting on the subject of
how to raise funds for the church, Bill had grown increasingly bitter. He would have preferred the subject to be how

to raise funds for Bill Jones. Seated across the table from Pastor Raymond Ortlund, he shared his problem and the disappointment of the day.

"I can't understand why God let me down."

Pastor Ortlund cheerfully replied, "Bill, don't be premature. You said you had until just before midnight. You still have almost five and one-half hours."

"Yes, Ray, but checks come in only during business hours."

Pastor Ortlund refused to go along with him. "God is open for business twenty-four hours a day," he replied.

Bill had an appointment to discuss a project with a client at 8:30, but no money would be involved there, so when the church meeting ended at 7:30, he had a little time to visit a friend.

"This man knew the Scriptures better than I did, and I wanted to find out why my prayer hadn't been answered," says Bill. "So I phoned Eagle Rock, where he then lived in the smallest home I had ever seen. It was so small that when you turned the door knob, you rearranged the furniture. He told me to come right over."

Bill immediately began to unload his problem of the overdraft and how upset he was about his unanswered prayer. He never did get to the part about how much money he needed.

With each word, Bill's host began to grin more broadly. Hardly a sympathetic attitude, thought Bill. Suddenly his host got up and, without explanation, walked out the front door. Several minutes later he came back, still grinning, and handed Bill a check.

"This is yours to keep," he said.

Bill glanced at the check, written in favor of William Converse Jones in the amount of $600. He was so astonished, he could not speak, although his mouth moved to ask the obvious questions.

His host, still smiling, explained, "Bill, a few months ago, my wife and I decided to live on faith and trust in the Lord, rather than rely on money in the bank. We prayed to God about how we shold use the money, and He told us we were to give it to you, but not immediately."

Now Bill leaned forward, too intrigued to ask questions. His host continued, "When I left you a few minutes ago, I had heard my wife's Volkswagen pull into the driveway. We prayed together to ask the Lord if this was the right time to give you the money. He told us *yes*."

"But why did you make out the check for six hundred dollars?" Bill asked.

His host laughed, "For a very practical reason. That's the exact amount we have in the bank!"

Sometimes we have no hesitancy about going to God for a relatively small amount, such as $600, as Bill Jones did, but we would never dare ask Him for vast sums.

That was not the problem of an acquaintance, a Los Angeles businessman. He dared ask for a miracle—a $14 million miracle—in a matter of days, to keep his company and shareholders from going under.

His firm had an excellent potential, but had overextended and run into a period of tight money. Everywhere he went, he was turned down. It seemed he had talked to every money source he knew in Los Angeles and Denver, but every source had dried up or failed to see that his business projections were real.

He prayed as he never had before. Only a miracle could save the company.

"God, I need a miracle right now, a fourteen-million-dollar miracle."

To do his part in the miracle, he retraced his steps, phoning or seeing every person who had already rejected him. Again, he was turned down.

Then, in total desperation, he spent an hour on his knees, praying. All of a sudden, he heard a clear voice ring through his mind. It said, "Fly to Denver tomorrow morning!"

"But, God, I've been there and have been turned down by everybody, just as I have in Southern California."

Again the voice instructed him, "Fly to Denver tomorrow morning."

"What am I supposed to do when I get to Denver?" he kept asking himself. "See the same old people and get the same old rejections?"

But he obeyed instructions.

On the already crowded aircraft, he found two side-by-side empty seats. Just as he had settled in comfortably, he noticed a giant of a man lumbering down the aisle, with an eye on the seat beside him.

The fellow must have been six foot five tall, poorly concealing about two hundred and forty pounds in a rich, gray, Harris tweed jacket. His thick, black, and neatly trimmed beard made him look as if he had come out of the pages of the Old Testament.

Moving over a bit in his own seat, the businessman welcomed the stranger. Soon they were talking.

"What brings you to Denver?" the stranger asked.

"My company has a great future, and I'm going to raise money to tide us over and permit us to expand." Then my acquaintance asked, "Why are *you* going to Denver?"

The man said, "I invest for a mutual fund. I'm going to Denver to look into a firm that needs expansion capital."

"How much do you have to invest?"

The answer shook him, "Fourteen million!"

"This is almost uncanny," replied my acquaintance. "That's the exact amount my company needs."

From that point on, it was as if the two had known each other all their lives.

They didn't stay long in Denver—only for lunch—taking

the next flight back to Los Angeles to work out final plans for the transaction.

God had worked a $14 million miracle that has turned my acquaintance's company into one of the most successful in its field.

9 Who Says You Can't?

"On the next day, she bought paint, brushes, and canvases and started. What she saw emerge on the canvas left her in awe."

Excuses, excuses, excuses!

"I never could understand mathematics."

"I guess I'm too old."

"You can't do anything without special training and education."

"Women still don't have a chance!"

Take a close look at yourself. Are you better at making alibis about your shortcomings, frustrations, and unhappiness than at taking positive action to correct these conditions?

If you've done everything humanly possible to help yourself and have failed, take heart. You can still turn to God for a miracle, as many have.

My friend Joe Stupak, whom you met in the chapter "Invisible Protectors," is a living example of somebody who admitted shortcomings and went right to the top, to God, for assistance.

An exciting thing happened to him while he was a California Institute of Technology student. One of his courses was so far out and esoteric that he felt the instructor was talking a foreign language that he had never heard before, let alone understood. He was fearful that he would fail so miserably that the course would annihilate his grade average.

What to do? He cast himself upon the Lord.

"That was an amazing time," admits Joe. "The Lord taught me something in that state that I couldn't have learned by any other means.

"The final exam was to be held in the middle of the term, because the instructor was going to be gone at the end of the term, to attend a conference somewhere.

"I had been praying, 'Lord, please give me some way to pass this course.'

"It seemed so impossible. I didn't understand anything about it. That day I walked into the class, and the Lord seemed to put His hand on me. I didn't even recognize the symbols the things were written in.

"I started working on the test, along with a room full of other people. The first question was really simple. I thought, 'The instructor must have put this in the test so that he could give a couple of points to the students like me, for just writing their names on the paper.'

"The next question was pretty easy, too. I was surprised. The third question was a little more difficult, but not much, and then I turned the page to the fourth question. Now this question wasn't like anything I had ever seen before, but it wasn't difficult at all. In fact, I was able to write it out immediately. It was interesting, but very simple.

"And I turned the page, and there were no more questions. I knew there was something wrong, because this kind of test usually runs about two hours. And I had taken only about twenty minutes. So I went up to the instructor and asked if I could have the rest of the test. 'I must be missing a big section.'

"He looked it over, a peculiar smile on his face, and said, 'No. That's all there is.' "

Joe went back to his desk, sat down and tried to find out

what was wrong. Maybe he didn't understand the questions at all. Yet that didn't seem to be it. So he got up, turned in his exam, and walked out of the room after one-half hour.

"That was the first time I ever received a special honor given to students at Caltech who do well on a test and walk out early," admits Joe. "Everybody boos and hisses."

The next day Joe walked into class with fear and trepidation. It had all been *too* easy. The instructor signaled him to come over and said, "Joe, would you mind talking with me for just a minute after class?"

Joe immediately began to tremble inwardly.

"Oh-oh, this is it. I'm going to get booted out of the class."

It bothered him throughout the session, because he had to pass the course in order to graduate that year.

"After class I went up to the instructor, who began looking over my test paper.

" 'Joe, you did very well. In fact, it's *perfect*. And there's something I want to ask you about: this last question. Nobody has *ever* solved this problem before. It was put in the test because the room was full of famous experts in the field.'

"He later told me that there were people in that class who were qualified to teach us, so he asked if I would please explain what I had done."

But Joe didn't know what he had done.

"I looked over the problem. Yes, I had written it, but I couldn't read it. The instructor let me off the hook. 'Look, Joe, I think I can more or less follow what you've done, but will you find some way of proving that this is the right answer?'

"I spent the next two weeks working on a big analog computer, setting up the problem to prove that this was really the right solution.

"And it was!

"What a demonstration this was of the first chapter of

James, verse five, 'If any of you lack wisdom, let him ask of God, that giveth to all men liberally, and upbraideth not; and it shall be given him.' ''

There are no strings attached to this offer. By the mere asking for wisdom, we acknowledge that we lack it and are resigned that the only way we'll get more is through God. Of course, we need a follow through of faith. We must expect Him to give it to us and keep on expecting until He has done so.

Charles Nielson, of the Apostolic Faith Mission in the Republic of South Africa has been a missionary for more than forty-three years among various tribes—the Bantus, Masai and Kikuyus—and his organization has started to verify, record, and attempt to understand why miracles happen.

A basic reason for miracles happening, he says is the "childlike but dynamic faith" of the natives and missionaries.

"There's no mystery to miracles. People just accept the Bible as written. There are no whys, wheres, and what fors."

Illustrating the point, Nielson tells the unusual story of a man named Joseph, who longed to be a more effective teacher of the Bible but had a severe handicap. One day he appealed to the missionary, "Overseer, God is using me, but I cannot read. I've never been to school. My wife has to read the Bible to me, and I have to remember the Scriptures. Quite often I forget and become embarrassed in front of my people who can read. Why don't you ask the Lord to teach me to read the Bible?"

Nielson nodded. "Sure, let's pray."

They prayed a very simple prayer, and the man went home.

"About three months later, I visited his kraal (hut) and he was sitting outside, with a Bible on his lap," relates Nielson. "A group of Africans were seated in a circle around him. Some had Bibles, and he was reading from the Bible."

Until that moment, Nielson had forgotten the prayer for him, and, in excitement hurried over.

"Now, Joseph, what happened?"

"Oh, you know, overseer, after we prayed together, I just went home and took my wife's Bible, and I started reading, and I've been reading ever since."

This is not meant to imply that schooling isn't necessary. God expects us to educate ourselves. As it has been said, "Pray as if you cannot work, and work as if you cannot pray!"

In response to our petitions, God can deliver specifically what we request, or, if we ask in general, what He knows we need in any or every circumstance.

When the late R. G. LeTourneau asked God into his life, he invited in the wisdom of the universe. A man of better-than-average intelligence but little formal education, Bob LeTourneau developed the abilities of his genius. His inventions of heavy machinery revolutionized the earth-moving industry.

He maintained that man, without God in his life, could not possibly receive the novel ideas that man with God receives. His hundreds of patents tend to bear out this point of view.

God's ideas are more and more available to us when we link our minds and hearts with Him. Pastor Ralph Wilkerson tells about one of the ushers at Melodyland Christian Center who, through prayer, was given a flash of inspiration for an invention which cleans up ocean oil slicks.

Several years ago, a junior accountant in a vast multinational firm prayed specifically for a way to do his work more efficiently and save his company money.

A born-again Christian, he received an input for simplifying accounting procedures. It was an easy-to-implement system and saved the company hundreds of thousands of dollars. Not long after, he was vaulted from obscurity to prominence, to become treasurer of the firm. He is now international vice president.

Often a single sound idea can revolutionize a business and a person's life.

Foster G. McGaw built the gigantic American Hospital Supply Company on a biblical principle. So poor that he had to drop out of high school because his churchman father could no longer support him, he founded a company on the idea of going the extra mile.

"Leave more than you get," he told his salesmen. "What you can do for the hospital people that we are not paid for will do more good than anything else we are paid to do."

The firm grew miraculously.

Christian business counselor and consultant Tom Frankhouser, of Pasadena, California, who started buying, renewing and reselling homes with only $200 and became a millionaire before he was thirty-five, calls his career turning point the day he invited Jesus into his life.

"I took literally the words about loving God and my neighbor as myself and put it into practice in business. I was then manager of the Lompoc, California, office of Beneficial Finance and did everything in my power to find ways for helping people who needed to qualify for a loan.

"Out of the thousands of people to whom I issued loans, I never had one person who went bankrupt and failed to pay the office. Most impressive of all, several of my greatest investment opportunities in real estate came through persons to whom I made loans."

Born in poverty in Attala County, Mississippi, and little educated, Wallace Johnson, a disheartened building-supplies salesman, in 1939 asked God to guide him in all things. That broke the logjam of his life.

An idea lit up his mind like a sunburst. He was to go into business for himself, building good quality, lowcost homes.

He shoestringed his first project through in Memphis, Tennessee, learning as he went. On-the-job education cost him heavily. He came out of the first house with only $181 in profit. Soon he was building an average of one thousand homes a year.

Today he is chairman of the board of Holiday Inns of America, the world's largest motel chain, with 280,000 units in 1,700 inns in 56 nations. The company has more than the aggregate of any five of the other leading motel chains.

Operating many companies, and active in numerous Christian organizations, Johnson has a schedule and work-load that are unreal. To keep up with everything, he has asked God for the ability to do the impossible. And this has been granted.

He can carry on a telephone conversation, dictate letters to his secretary while the person on the other end of the line is speaking (retaining the gist of his or her remarks), and write letters or reports in longhand at the same time.

It is standard practice for Johnson to work on eight activities at a given time, moving from one project to the other without mental gearshifting.

One of the most spectacular instances of miraculous communication with God is that of Father Bruce Medaris, mentioned earlier. In World War II he was General Medaris, in charge of military logistics under General Omar Bradley.

During a telecast of the PTL Club, he described getting on a one-on-one conversational basis with the Lord (further elaborated in his biography by Gordon Harris, *A New Command*) and asking for God's help in the Allied cause against Nazi Germany.

". . . I began to put up decisions at night before I went to bed, and in the morning there were clear answers. Some were ridiculous. One of them almost got me fired.

"If it hadn't been for Bradley, I would have been, because the amount of welding rod we were to take with us to the continent—the answer the Lord gave me—was ridiculous.

"We got a cable from Washington that said, 'There isn't that much in the United States. We've got to start factories to make it. I think this guy has flipped, and you'd better relieve him.'

"Bradley called me in, but by that time he was kind of used to my mysterious answers, and he apparently had a lot of confidence in me. He told me one time, 'As long as you are my ordnance officer, you will have the authority in your area. When I can't trust you for that, I'll relieve you.'

"So it was live or die . . . . Anyway, he said, 'Where did you get this figure?'

"I said, 'I don't know, but that's how much I've got to have.' "

Bradley backed him, and they got the welding rod. When the Allies invaded Normandy, they couldn't break through the thick hedgerows. A young man in an armored-cavalry regiment invented a set of forks that were attached to the front of tanks. These would demolish the hedgerows. General Bradley gave Medaris a demonstration of the invention and told him he wanted 800 tanks equipped with them.

Medaris sent his men to the beach to extricate steel tetrahedrons which the Germans had sunk into the ocean to tear out the bottoms of invading boats. These were cut up and, with the welding rod, they welded them to the tank fronts.

"We got together the welding rod that I'd buried around the place, so that nobody could see how ridiculous the amount was," explains Medaris. "We turned out eight hundred tanks, and there weren't one hundred pounds of welding rod left in the whole place.

"So the Lord knew what was going to happen."

Medaris soon asked for guidance on all major issues, " 'Lord, You know my problem for today. I have to have a decision.' I got so I kept a notebook by my bed. In the morning there was an answer that had to go down. The Lord quickly proved Himself faithful."

Miracles of the Lord even extend to those who have no special abilities or training for the kind of work they wish to do. One of the most remarkable concerns a lady interviewed by Jim Bakker, host of TV's PTL Club.

Stavritza "Momma" Zacharion, who is from Greece and a member of the Greek Orthodox Church, had prayed constantly on a personal basis with the Lord, and one night, while she was asleep in her New York City apartment, she was wakened and saw somebody sitting in her chair near the bed.

She knew it was Jesus Christ. He told her He wanted her to be a missionary to spread the Gospel in Africa.

Momma Stavritza prayed all night for guidance. She didn't know much about missionary work, Africa, or specifically what she was going to do when she got there. One thing she knew for sure: She was going to obey instructions.

At age fifty-seven, Momma Stavritza flew to Nairobi, Kenya. There she found a need for a church to accommodate converts to Christianity and others whom she hoped to help find Jesus Christ as their personal Saviour.

Who ever heard of an up-in-years woman, in a strange land, and with little money, attempting single-handedly to raise funds for a one-thousand-seat church and getting it built?

Such an assignment is a monumental task for an entire

committee of a church which has a congregation of money
earners, but Momma Stavritza figured she didn't need much
more help. After all, she had the most powerful Ally in the
universe.

In her broken English, she appealed everywhere for
funds, and everywhere she was turned down. It was then
she realized how inadequate she was for her job. She hadn't
even been educated for a job so that she could earn money
for her church.

One night, in total hopelessness, she cried out to the Lord
for talent and ability to paint religious pictures that would
command huge sums for the church construction.

"My dear Jesus," she prayed, "I want to be a painter,
not to be rich and have a mink coat—just to help the poor
churches and monasteries. Please make me a painter!"

On the next day, she bought paint, brushes, and can-
vasses and started. What she saw emerge on the canvas left
her in awe. She had been given the rare ability to paint
gloriously, something she had never done in her life. Her
magnificent religious paintings—accomplished without ego,
with full credit to the Lord—sell readily and have brought
astonishing sums.

Momma Stavritza got her church all right, after perform-
ing other kinds of work she had never before done or been
trained for: the architecture, construction supervision, and
even laboring.

The church is a thing of beauty and filled with people, for
which Momma thanks her silent Partner.

10 The Necessary Ingredient—

Helplessness

". . . I cannot handle being burned, being childless, and being widowed—two out of three, maybe, but not all three."

Paradoxical as it may seem, few human qualities are more helpful than helplessness, in making way for miracles.

Only when we have come to the end of our resources can we tap His. Only then can we let go and let God.

Today, many individuals, many couples, many families have reached the dead end of human potential. Yet the very situation which, to them, spells despair, can present opportunity.

One of the most devastating things a mother or father can discover is hypodermic-needle marks on the arm of a son or daughter. Such things are supposed to happen to other parents—not to them.

But it did happen to Floyd and Zoe. Hank, their son in his late teens, was hooked on heroin.

After the initial shock, tears, and depression, they tried in every human way to help—they and their family doctor—but Hank didn't seem to want help.

Absent for days at a time, he skipped meals, lost weight, and his skin assumed a sickly pallor.

"Oh, God," cried out Zoe in desperation, "if we could only make him see what he's doing to himself."

All at once, she realized that she had unconsciously called out to God.

God *was* the answer.

She and Floyd did something they had not done in years—prayed on their knees together.

"God, in the name of Jesus, make Hank see what he's doing to his body, his future, his life!"

Then Zoe heard an authoritative voice, "Keep on praying."

She glanced at Floyd.

"Did you hear that?"

"Hear what?" asked Floyd.

"A voice told me to keep on praying."

Zoe and Floyd prayed long and hard to Jesus to work a miracle on Hank's life.

A few days later, Hank went into the bathroom and glanced into the mirror.

He gasped in horror.

What he saw chilled him as if an icicle had been driven into his heart.

The image in the mirror was not his own. It was a skull supported by a skeleton.

"Nothing I've ever seen shook me up as much as that!" he says.

God had provided the exact miracle for which Zoe had prayed. From that day, Hank lost all desire for narcotics and has enrolled in college.

Floyd and Zoe have rejoined their Christian church. They again believe in miracles, because Hank is a constant reminder that Jesus lives today, as He did yesterday and will forever.

Just as narcotics and alcohol are destroying many marriages, so is the desire to shake off adult responsibility and enjoy the "good and exciting life" on the outside.

The marriage of Carole and Rick Johnson, in the words of her mother, had been "a fine, delicate China cup that was made flawless. It was dropped and broken into a million pieces, irreparable by human hands . . . ."

Carole tells the whole story in a *Testimony* magazine article.

Rick had accepted a position as a junior civil engineer in the California Department of Water Resources, and Carole worked in a bank, until she gave birth to a beautiful daughter, Theresa.

Both Christians, Rick and Carole had been married by Pastor Donald Skaggs, Carole's father.

In these days it is not fashionable to believe Satan is real, and Carole lost sight of her Bible training on this subject. She became discontented and restless, and made excuses to skip going to church.

"Our apartment became a prison, and I began having feelings of being locked away, while the good and exciting things of life were passing me by."

For a year and one-half, while Rick spent off-work time studying for his master's degree in sanitary engineering, Carole, thirsting for independence, tried to subdue her rebellion. When it broke loose, she and Rick stopped communicating. Soon they were total strangers and decided that the only "natural" solution was divorce.

Carole readily gave up her home, husband, and daughter for freedom.

In no time, she was back in circulation, but, surprisingly, the partying soon wore thin, and she could no longer hide her loneliness, restlessness, and frustration. She sadly remembered the inner peace she once had in her life with the presence of God.

She wistfully recalled life with the husband and daughter

she had given up so easily. They could never be hers again! She also felt that she had given up the Lord, and that Satan was now dominating her life.

For two years pride kept her from admitting she had been wrong, and she grew increasingly miserable.

One night, while alone in her apartment doing dishes, she was frightened by a satanic attack: "I suddenly felt an invisible cloud hovering over the apartment. As it was slowly settling down, I felt a sudden panic . . . . I realized there wasn't a person who could help me in this situation . . . because I was dealing with the spiritual realm.

". . . I found myself in front of the bathroom mirror for hours, talking to myself, emptying out all the excuses I had ever used to keep me from surrendering my life to the Lord. Then this cloud lifted."

A week later the crushing cloud came down upon her, and she reacted in the same way. To get away from the apartment, she spent the weekend with her parents, out of town. As she was getting ready to drive back to Los Angeles, her father, knowing she was troubled, put his arms around her, told her he loved her, and asked if there was anything he and her mother could do for her.

Carole broke down and described her experiences of satanic oppression. Her father soothed her.

"You know, Carole, there is Someone who loves you, cares for you, and knows your needs better than I myself, and that's Jesus! If you ever experience that again, remember you have a Friend right there with you. You can turn to Him, and tell Him all about it."

One night the cloud came again.

"This time I knew I wasn't going to escape," says Carole. "I was gripped with the fear of being crushed by this invisible cloud . . . . In desperation I called out for the Lord to forgive me. If He still wanted this life of mine, after I had messed it up, it was one hundred percent His. I cried out, 'Jesus, help me.' Instantly the cloud lifted and I was filled with His beautiful peace . . . . Now I knew what it was really like to be a liberated woman! I burst into a heavenly language of praise and thanked the Lord for setting me free!"

Beautiful weeks followed, and into Carole's mind came an idea that kept repeating: Happiness could come only from being the wife of Rick and the mother of Theresa!

But would they take her back?

She phoned Rick in Milwaukee, Wisconsin, to tell him how the Lord had changed her life. He was pleased, but didn't want to discuss the possibility of a reconciliation.

Several months went by, and no word came from Rick. Carole quit her job in Los Angeles and went back home to her parents.

Carole had no way of knowing what that action meant to Rick. His independent wife had moved back with her parents.

Rick and Carole were soon remarried by her father. The fine, delicate China cup that had been broken into a million pieces, irreparable by human hands, had experienced a miracle. God had taken the minute fragments and fused them so artfully that the repair couldn't be seen by human eyes.

Now the cup is even more beautiful and stronger than it was originally.

A far greater stress than divorce came to Diane Bringgold, of Ventura, California—a stress that few people can handle without help from God.

On a flight from northern California, the Bringgold's Cessna 210 smashed into a mountaintop in the fog. Diane's attorney husband and her three children were killed instantly. She and a married couple, the Dixons, were hurled onto a ridge. Her face was badly burned and, she knew, disfigured. Desolate and depressed over the loss of her family and even her beauty, so important in her life, she also lost the will to live.

In a national television interview with Pat Robertson on the 700 Club, she said, "Burns were one injury that terrified me. I have no tolerance for pain, and I'm an abject physical coward."

Her friends who were in the crash couldn't see Diane where she lay. They called to her.

"I didn't answer, because if they didn't know I was alive, maybe the rescuers wouldn't look for me, and I could remain hidden until I died of exposure."

She didn't have a chance to follow the plan.

". . . Suddenly there on the mountain, about ten feet away, was a white-robed figure. (Sometimes people say, 'Well, describe Him,' but I really can't. He was tall. I knew it was a man, but it was foggy, and He wasn't dispelling the fog. I simply knew it was Christ.) I think one reason He appeared to me robed in white was that was the way I would have expected Him to look.

"So He said, 'Diane, it is not up to you to decide whether to live or die. That is My decision to make.' "

Since Diane is a hardheaded lady, Diane said, "That's easy for You to say, Lord, but I cannot handle being burned, being childless, and being widowed—two out of the three maybe, but not all three.

"I wasn't really trying to bargain with Him. He could have restored my family. He could have healed me instantly, but I wasn't expecting that. I was just trying to impress upon Him that it was the whole situation I couldn't cope with.

"He didn't say anything after that first comment that it wasn't my decision, so I continued, 'If You want me to live, I will give You my life. I will give You these problems, and You will have to cope with the loneliness, with the pain and with the grief, because I can't. And that's where it is.'

"If we really turn our lives and our problems, big or small, over to the Lord, He takes care of them. He took them, and still didn't say anything, but He has given me a beautiful gift: the gift of faith. And I knew that He had taken these things on, that everything would be all right. As suddenly as He appeared, He was no longer there. I came out of my hiding place, called back to the Dixons, and shortly thereafter we were found and rescued.''

Previously Diane had had a close relationship with the Lord, but she was a strong and cool person and had never before run into anything she couldn't handle, so she had never asked His help.

''And now I look back and think, *As good as things were, life still would have been so much easier if I had just put Him in charge, because I literally have not worried about anything since that time.*''

God guided her all the way through. She seemed to be insulated from unbearable pain.

''There were times in the hospital when I turned and asked, 'Why me, Lord?' The Lord really helped me, because He reminded me that, for a Christian, death is not the worst thing that can happen. And I'm really thankful that He took my family to Him without their suffering. It would have been harder to watch them suffer.

''I had about one tenth of the pain that I expected to have. I did have pain. Physical therapy was excruciating, and some of the procedures prior to grafting were very painful, but out of twenty-four hours, there were maybe four hours of intense pain. So most of the time, I was comfortable.

''I've had seven more surgeries and have had no post-operative pain, and I'm still sensitive to pain. I've had routine dental work done, and my dentist will testify that I am still a physical coward.

''Many people would think that, out of my own need, I had dreamed the vision up. I would have thought that, if someone had told me of it before it happened. I went to a prayer group in Chico and told them what had happened.

And one of the women there said, 'I really think the Lord is going to use this, and you are going to go out and testify to what He has done in your life and how great things are when you really can trust Him.'

"My answer was, 'I hope not.' But the Lord has made me want to share it."

Many individuals would have become resentful about the accident in many ways—not the least of these due to loss of physical attractiveness.

"The Lord has used my injuries in lots of ways," she admits. "I'm really thankful I was injured. It helps me to cope with the loss of my family. I had to pay a lot of attention to getting me well at first. He has used it to show me looks aren't all that important. I used to be really hung up on what I looked like.

"It has been fantastic to find out that people really do like me, no matter what I look like. I wore an elastic mask over my face, almost all of the time, for a year and one-half, to maintain constant pressure on the grafts, so they would heal smoothly. I looked like a bank robber. The Lord gave me a sense of humor about it; I made new friends even then, and they didn't know what I looked like. I might have looked horrible underneath my mask."

While Diane Bringgold knew there was a God to help her through the crisis, Allan Mayer, former officer and current board member of Oscar Mayer & Company, didn't even know that God exists.

"I never thought I'd need Him in my life. I never prayed with much earnestness or expectation and didn't go to church or read the Bible."

Everything was great: his health, finances, family, and friends. He and his wife even had a little daughter, something quite rare in the family. His brothers and one sister had eleven boys and only one girl.

A short time later, after he, his wife, and daughter moved

from Madison, Wisconsin, to Arizona, his elation turned to apprehension.

"In the spring of 1972, we noticed some physical changes in our daughter's face. Her eyelids started to droop, and she had a floating right eye that wouldn't focus. We had her examined. The original diagnoses were not alarming; we were told she just had an allergy and a simple muscular problem with her right eye that could likely be corrected with exercises."

Then the Mayers went back to Madison, their home for many years, where their daughter reached the climax of a serious illness, diagnosed as a brain tumor.

"We took her to a renowned medical institution, where she underwent a five-hour operation in order to remove the tumor. It was located so deeply that this was impossible. The neurosurgeon, however, got a snip of it for a biopsy, which revealed it as a malignant brain tumor."

Doctors said all they could do was give her cobalt radiation, which might help temporarily, but which would never cure the tumor.

"I was so depressed and desperate that I didn't know which way to turn. I started going to the hospital chapel, praying on my knees and also went to an old church in town to pray. I can remember seeing a beautiful stained-glass window behind the altar, portraying an adult with three children, but wasn't even sure the adult was Jesus. He had His hand on the head of a little blond-haired girl who resembled our daughter. I just prayed to Him that He was indicating that He would heal our girl."

For the first time in his life, Allan Mayer was faced with a truly hopeless situation—something that nothing in his power could change.

"The doctors gave her only a few months to live, and her appearance was so terrible I could hardly look at her. She was shaven bald for the craniotomy and had a long scar down the back of her head. Because of the medication she took, her face was puffed out like a pumpkin, as was her stomach. She was hallucinating and had three major things wrong with her eyes.''

After seven weeks at the hospital, they flew back to Arizona, where Mayer continued his new Christian pursuits of praying and reading the Bible.

''I, the former agnostic, became convinced there was a God and Jesus Christ. In a bedroom, I got down on my knees and received Jesus Christ as my Lord and Saviour.

''Now that I look back on it, that was the greatest decision I ever made. There was no particular emotional sensation at the time, as some people experience. It was just a gradual blossoming and growth in the love of Jesus and my faith in Him. The spiritual healing that came over me was the most important thing that can happen to anyone— something I so desperately needed all my life.''

After intercessory prayers by friends and relatives throughout the country and by Allan himself, his daughter's condition began to improve in November, 1972.

''In my prayers, I asked the Lord to heal her of the drooping eyelids. It was beautiful. In a few days, her eyes were wide open again—just like two full moons.''

Mayer didn't want to ask the Lord for too much at one time.

''I prayed on the installment plan,'' he says. ''I waited a month to ask the Lord to heal our daughter of her floating right eye and double vision. And again, the same thing happened.''

From that point on, his daughter improved in many respects. Three years later, they took her back to the clinic for a checkup.

''The doctors could hardly believe she was the same little girl who had been given only a few months to live. She had a full battery of tests, including a brain scan, which is very revealing. They told us that all her tests showed no signs of her former tumor.''

Mayer told the brain surgeon how his daughter had improved after prayer. The surgeon's last words were:

"Allan, it's a miracle!"

Al Mayer now gives all glory to God and believes that "all good and bad things work together for good for those who love the Lord." (*See* Romans 8:28.)

His life has taken an about-face in many respects.

"Before I received the Lord, I was periodically critical, negative, bitter, cynical, and sarcastic—even hateful toward certain people and situations. I praise and thank God for removing these traits from me and for replacing them with much better desires and activities.

"In past times, I never read the Bible, because I thought it was just a compilation of nice fairylike tales—irrelevant and boring. Now I believe the Bible is God's infallible Word, that everything in it is true, and that it's definitely our navigation chart for life; it has all the answers that we'll ever need to any problems."

Like Al Mayer, Melvin Purvis, Jr., learned that helplessness is a necessary ingredient for a miracle.

Miserable, dejected, depressed, emotionally ill, Purvis felt that there was no hope for him. Life had betrayed him at every turn. *Why continue to live?* he asked himself. All that seemed to be left was suicide.

Fearing for his life, Purvis's friends removed every hand gun from his home.

Often he wondered what influence, over the years, had driven him to this point of desperation. He had been born into what society labeled "a good family." His father, Melvin Purvis, had been one of the most famous G-men of the 1930s—the officer who had shot John Dillinger, one of the era's most wanted men, outside the Biograph Theater in Chicago. He had single-handedly captured another legendary criminal, Pretty Boy Floyd.

Melvin, Jr., lived in the shadow of his celebrated and

highly publicized father. Even in his early years, he was searching for answers. The people in the country churches seemed to have a reality that he never had. He had been taught by intimation that that sort of religious experience was for uneducated, simple country people.

Education! Maybe that was the secret. So he attended college.

"I had been told that the more education you got, the happier you were bound to be. So I began a headlong pursuit of knowledge. The Bible calls this: 'Ever learning, and never able to come to the knowledge of the truth.' I pursued the poets, the playwrights, the great writers, the psychiatrists, the philosophers. And, yet, something was missing. It did not fill the emptiness in me. I felt sometimes that I had been tricked. Even with more education, I didn't feel fulfilled personally.

"There was a God-shaped hole in me, and I poured alcohol into it. I was an alcoholic drinker for eleven years. I finally reached the point where I would have to sober up or die. Confronted with such a challenge, I chose to get sober. I thought so much of myself, at the time, that I didn't want to lose myself.

"When I was twenty-eight years old, I began to see happiness through making money. The Bible says '. . . the love of money is the root of all evil: which while some coveted after, they have erred from the faith and pierced themselves through with many sorrows.' So the Bible says I was going to be pierced with many sorrows. And so it was.

"The more I made, the more successful I became, the more miserable I became, and that, again, was a puzzle to me, because the advertising people had promised me that if I made enough money, I was bound to be happy."

Soon he reached a certain pinnacle of success, sure that "some cloud of happiness would descend upon me at that point." It didn't happen. Instead, he began to have what's known as anxiety attacks. Several things triggered this.

"In my headlong quest for personal success and power, I had lost the ability to love anybody, especially myself.

"The anxiety attacks soon developed into what the medical world calls morbid-anxiety psychosis, and also manic depression.

"The doctor to whom I went—I learned later—diagnosed me as hopeless, and if you read the medical books, which I've done since, you will know that there is no return from what I had.

"I had lost all hope. I would stay home and cry all afternoon and grind my fingernails in my palms and shake. I knew I was gone. I knew I had met a force bigger than my willpower and my intellect.

"In the midst of this, a man—a businessman, not a preacher—drove eight hours in the night to see me, and there were some holy coincidences that brought him there.

"He sat down at the kitchen table and told me about a man named Jesus Christ who died for me, who loved me so much that He carried my guilt and my sins away on the cross.

"I looked at that man. I had lost so much weight. I was losing ground and knew there was no hope, and I said, 'I'm going crazy, but he's got to be crazy, too. I wish he'd get out of here.' And he left.

"Two weeks later, I lay down on the bed with my old 30-30 deer rifle. I loaded and cocked the rifle up under my head, and reached out to pull the trigger. The phone rang. It was an old friend who wanted to know how I was. I was very short with him. I lay back on the bed but didn't bring the rifle back to my head, and I slept that night. During the night an unseen presence was in that room, and two things were ministered to me from outside myself. (I now know this to be God, the Holy Spirit.)

"One was that my problem was not my troubles—and I had plenty of troubles—my problem was sin, plain old sin. And I had two choices. I could get simple, humble, and healed, or I could stay clever and die.''

He didn't quite know what to make of this, but he slept the rest of the night. At dawn, he was up and driving his car. In a South Carolina town, he pulled to a stop when a traffic light turned red, and, as he waited there, he realized he was beaten, completely finished.

"The old, smart Mel had come to the end of me. There was no hope. I said a simple prayer. I know that prayer as if it were yesterday: 'All right, Jesus, You promised to be with me. I need You now.' And the car filled with a bright light, and I saw the figure of Jesus Christ, standing with His arms outstretched to me.

"I was instantly and perfectly healed. I knew something then. I didn't know what the Scripture said, but I knew then that somebody had died and somebody new had come into being.

"I only found out months later that God had said, 'If you're in Christ, you are a new creation. Old things are passed away. Behold all things are become new.' '' (*See* 2 Corinthians 5:17.)

Purvis indicates that God does not come to everybody in the same way. Most of the time it is not as a vision, not dramatic. It is usually quiet and not even sensed but must be accepted by faith, as the Bible says.

Is mental illness the will of God?

"No," says Purvis. "Mental illness and darkness are not the will of God for His people. Jesus is in the healing business. He said, 'If you follow Me, you shall not walk in darkness.' ''

Purvis says the secret to healing is coming to Jesus with a heart contrite for sins, asking to be born again, and accepting the fact that you are born again.

The experience of Melvin Purvis, Jr., shows that in hopelessness there is hope and in helplessness there is help.

The word *hopeless* is commonly used to describe the

condition of homosexuals. It is said that there is no cure for homosexuality. Is it true or false?

"False," insists Pastor Paul Olson, who runs a crisis center connected with his church, in a theater in downtown Minneapolis, near the gay community.

Many gays have been permanently healed through the crisis center, he told Host Jim Bakker, and the audience for television's PTL Club.

A homosexual came in one Friday night to talk to the young people who are counselors.

"Most gays I know would rather not be gay, but most of us live a life of hopelessness," he said. "The church despises us, and there is no hope for us."

The counselors took the young man down into the prayer room and began to pray.

"There was an enormous manifestation of demon power," said Olson. "It took seven people to hold this young man down, and he had the body of a woman—a frail woman.

"In three hours of frothing at the mouth and cursing in unbelievable language, the vileness that came out of his mouth was unbelievable. After that time, God delivered that boy of seven demons. They came out of him one at a time. He stood up, completely liberated.

"Homosexuality is deeply entrenched in demon power. This fellow's father is a warlock in Dallas. He has come out of a home situation of evil power. He was a stripper in a homosexual nightclub, a female impersonator, and he prided himself on having a feminine body," says Olson.

This young man has since been at Midwest Challenge with Al Palmquist, and has been observed in a controlled environment. He is now in phase three of the program, and is living a life completely liberated from homosexuality; he is changing spiritually and emotionally after confessing his sins, asking forgiveness, and inviting Christ into his life.

Several other homosexuals have been cured in Olson's

church, and he is optimistic that the power of Jesus can drive out demons in homosexuals everywhere.

"I believe that homosexuality is not a sickness," insists Olson. "It is not an alternate life-style. Homosexuality is a sin. That's what the Bible says. It's not what I think, or what Anita Bryant thinks. It's what the Word of God says."

Olson offers hope to all who are involved in this kind of sin and are clouded over with hopelessness, to those who say, "This is the way I am. I've tried to quit, but there's no hope."

"But there is hope," says Olson.

And he has the evidence to prove it!

11 How to Play Your Part in Miracles

"Let's go ahead as far as we can in
the natural and expect God to take
over in the supernatural."

Awed by the overwhelming wonder and mystery of miracles, we tend to feel too small, inconsequential, and unworthy, to realize that we are essential to them.

In a sense, ". . . we are labourers together with God . . ." (1 Corinthians 3:9), partners in God's miracles—junior partners, but partners, nevertheless.

While God gives us the seed, we plant and water.

So it is today. So it was when Jesus attended the wedding feast of Cana. (*See* John 2:1–11.) Mary, mother of Jesus, brought her faith to the miracle of turning water into wine by telling Jesus, "They have no wine," indirectly asking Him for help with the host's problem.

Then she told the servants, "Whatsoever he saith unto you, do it."

The servants were obedient to Mary and Jesus, acting in faith that something was going to happen.

> Jesus saith unto them, Fill the waterpots with water.
> And they filled them up to the brim. And he saith unto
> them, Draw out now, and bear unto the governor of the

feast. And they bare it. When the ruler of the feast had tasted the water that was made wine, and knew not whence it was: (but the servants which drew the water knew;) the governor of the feast called the bridegroom, And saith unto him, Every man at the beginning doth set forth good wine; and when men have well drunk, then that which is worse: but thou has kept the good wine until now.

When Jesus was going to feed the five thousand, He didn't say, "Stand over there and watch Me do My thing." He said, "How many loaves have you? Lay on the line what you've got. You're going to furnish the raw materials. You're going to be a partner with Me in this miracle."

Jesus' glory was not in doing it all by Himself. His glory was in making people like us His partners.

When Peter was going to walk on water, did Jesus hoist him out of the boat and put one foot ahead of the other? No. If He had, He would have made him a zombie, and Jesus is not in the zombie-making business. Peter could walk. He had to go as far as he could in the natural, then Jesus took over in the supernatural.

When God called me to start pastoring at the historic First Reformed Church of Mount Vernon, New York, I discovered that the city had suffered the greatest White Flight of any city in the four surrounding states, and that this once-affluent church with its classic Gothic architecture and stained-glass windows was left high and dry and all but deserted in a black ghetto—with few parishioners to support it.

Pat Robertson, president of the Christian Broadcasting Network, who was then my student pastor, said, "Harald, the first order of business is to restore this church, because people will come here and see the falling plaster and the corroding windows and conclude, 'It must be true. God is dead,' or, 'These people must not enjoy, know, or love

God, or they wouldn't let this church fall into such sad disrepair.' It is a terrible witness." And he said, "Let's go ahead as far as we can in the natural and expect God to take over in the supernatural."

So we went for a contractor to give an estimate. After looking at the lofty ceilings with the huge crossbeams, he said, "The ceilings are so high that just to put up the interior scaffolding will cost five thousand dollars."

Our total income that year had been $11,600, and we ended up $1,500 in the red, so that didn't leave much for putting up the scaffolding, not to mention doing the work. It would cost $25,000 to complete the job, including restoration of the stained-glass windows. Fortunately, the exterior was in perfect condition.

Well, by getting the estimate, we had gone as far as we could in the natural, so the next step was up to God. Every time we went over there, Pat and I thanked God that He was in the process of restoring this church to His glory.

Months later, we got the news. A ninety-three-year-old agnostic, a total stranger whom no one in our church knew—he had never even been inside the door or had shown a flicker of interest—on his deathbed had made out his will, leaving us $25,000.

So from that point on, I found it easy to believe in miracles. Whenever I was stumped and up against some big financial problem, I would go over to the church, now restored to greater beauty than ever before. I would look at that exquisite interior, and God would say to me, "I am the Lord thy God, which brought thee out of the land of Egypt: open thy mouth wide, and I will fill it." (Psalms 81:10.)

It was as if He were saying, "I am the Lord God who made a ninety-three-year-old agnostic on his deathbed make out his will, leaving you $25,000. In other words, on the basis of My track record, believe Me for even greater things."

Like so many individuals with a worthy project, Syvelle Phillips had great faith, but no capital to get started.

An eminently successful minister of the First Assembly of God Church in Santa Ana, California—a great missionary church—Pastor Phillips sensed in the Spirit that he should help hurry along Bible translation into all tongues of the earth, by forming Evangel Bible Translators.

It would have been financially convenient if he could have straddled the fence, staying with his church and, at the same time, heading the new organization, but he knew that wouldn't work.

So, after seven rewarding years, he willingly turned from the known quantities of security to insecurity, resigning from his pastorate and giving up his home, good pay, and numerous understanding friends.

One gets to know God better under such circumstances.

His first act of faith in the new project was to take a bold step: rent an office when the organization had no financial reserve and not a cent of income. He owned no office equipment, not much of anything on the material level, but he had the most powerful Partner in the universe. He asked God to add His resources to Evangel Bible Translators.

Then the missing parts began to fall into place. Out of a clear sky (that of his Partner) his former church gifted him with an almost unheard of severance pay—six months' salary—to remove some of the bumps from the transition period.

A missionary organization assumed part of his secretary's salary, a major roadblock, and leased an IBM typewriter for the office.

It seemed that every problem became a solution. The church had leased a new car for him, and now he was faced with heavy payments: $172.00 per month. As he was contemplating some other arrangement a man gave him a Lincoln Continental with only 35,000 miles on the odometer. He was able to cancel the car lease. Friends who own a service station offered him all the gasoline he required.

One morning, as he was about to leave for his unfurnished office, he said to his wife, "God knows I can't sit on the floor to do my work."

God knew that and did something right away to help His partner.

A friend with whom Phillips was having lunch that day, asked, "Syvelle, if God gave you what you prayed for this morning, what would it be?"

"A desk and chair!"

The friend smiled broadly, and said, "Would you believe I have a new desk and chair that have been in storage for four years? You're welcome to them."

Syvelle Phillips got immediate delivery of his desk and chair—and a bonus: two matching side chairs and a new AM-FM stereo set.

Each day brought new surprises: adding machines, file cabinets, other furniture, and a $3,000 reproduction machine.

Friends wanted him to forget about financial matters and concentrate on his important work of Bible translation, so they provided him with living expenses and money for travel.

Syvelle Phillips is pleased with the progress of Evangel Bible Translators. At this writing, he is working toward starting a badly needed West Coast school for training future translators in linguistics and in preparing Bibles in languages for primitive people.

He's certain the project will work out well, not only because he is doing everything he can, but because he has a Partner who accomplishes the many things that Syvelle can't.

If *you* need a miracle—as Syvelle Phillips and Pat Robertson and I did—a job, a car, a home, or some other

major or minor thing, you should know that God expects
you to play your part.

Angelina Foglio understands that fact even better now
than she did some years ago when she called upon God to
provide a miracle for a small but important matter to her.

Frank Foglio, of Fontana, California, her son, has wit-
nesses to verify the extraordinary happening to Momma
Foglio, a true believer in every word of the Bible.

Momma Foglio was caught short on supply of a certain
food. She had what seemed to be an insurmountable task of
cooking a spaghetti dinner for her family of twelve and six
guests, eighteen in all, with only one-quarter pound of
spaghetti.

Now anyone who has ever cooked spaghetti knows that a
pound of spaghetti can serve no more than four or five
persons. That means that something like four to five pounds
would be required to feed a mob of eighteen.

This lady of faith put the quarter of a pound of spaghetti
into her largest cooking utensil, in salted, boiling water, and
prayed with Bible in one hand and a spoon in the other,
stirring like crazy.

So what happened?

When the hungry eighteen were assembled, there was
more than enough spaghetti to eat, and overeat, and still
enough left for the family of twelve to dine on the next
evening.

In reading a book of this kind, it is possible to get the
impression that once you enter the miraculous, the dimension of miracles, you step from mountaintop to mountaintop.

Are there any failures?

Plenty of them.

At the beginning, you could have more failures than suc-
cesses. A baby learning to walk may be on his bottom as

much as on his feet. If he falls it is not serious, unless he just sits there.

We don't always get the asked-for miracle. God reserves the right to give us a better one. He also arranges timing, which may be entirely different than we expect.

Let's consider timing. Think about the wayside meadow that you see along the highway. One day cows are grazing there. Next time you drive by, you see a housing project. It seems so fast that you feel it's almost a miracle.

But a year or more of preparation and groundwork had to be done by the developer, the architect, and the contractor. Plans had to be reviewed and approved by city or county officials. Subcontractors had to be scheduled in and out before what seemed like a sudden surge of growth could take place.

Often miracles involve timing of different people and related events. So, until it all comes together, you've got to have faith.

The greatest best-seller of all times not only recounts miracles but promises them to you under several conditions. You must have gone as far as you can in the natural and, falling short, be aware that you need a miracle. Then you must have the faith to claim it. At this point, God will take over in the supernatural and perform a miracle.

Each miracle builds your faith for the next miracle—a greater one. So you can go from faith to faith, from glory to glory, and from strength to strength.

12 They Came Back to Tell

> "There was not even a scratch on
> her head . . . . The doctors looked
> at the blanket, all soaked with blood,
> and they could not understand it."

Once upon a time, death was considered final.

Then, almost two thousand years ago, a man from Nazareth, Jesus Christ, changed that sort of thinking with several electrifying miracles which couldn't have happened, but did.

Today, too, people are being raised from the dead and by the same person, Jesus, through God's Holy Spirit. The one difference is that human intercessors form the link to Jesus and His miraculous power.

Again scoffers are saying it can't happen, but it is.

Individuals of all walks and ages have had the experience of dying and being brought back to life by prayers.

As the result of a violent accident, race driver Jan Opperman came to the end and found a new beginning. During the Hoosier 100 at Indianapolis, he had moved from sixth to second place on turn one and had been putting pressure on the race leader, Johnny Parsons, for fifty laps.

On the fifty-first lap, Parsons's car spun wide, and Opperman's car flipped over Parsons's left front wheel. Driver Chuck Gurney came high in turn three and couldn't avoid Opperman's car. Crash!

Opperman, from California and now living in Montana, tells of the event:

"In the crash where I was wiped out, I had a little better car than the leader and was running carefully behind him to save my tires, because if you run too hard at the start of the race, you don't have tires by the end, and they only pay for the last lap. They don't pay for how you do early in the race.

"I figured to go to the front at the halfway. They had just put out the halfway sign, so I decided to go after him. I was passing when he spun out, which happens a lot on a dirt track. He spun around sideways. My right front ran over his left front, which flipped me upside down at over one hundred miles an hour.

". . . A car that was running in sixth place came my way with nowhere to go, and he just drove into my cockpit. We don't have a closed cockpit. His bumper hit my helmet and caved it in. The impact spun me around in the cockpit. It caved my head in, put a hole in my head and got to my brain."

As soon as the crowd formed around him, the track doctor took a close look at him, checked for heartbeat and respiration, shook his head, and said to no one in particular, "He's dead."

Opperman had come to the track with a fellow driver, his wife, and a sister in the Lord—spiritual people from Elwood, Indiana, who had faith in prayer power.

Like thousands of others in the crowd, Queenie and Linda were watching the race when they had a premonition of disaster. Suddenly they became aware that God was asking them to go to the corner of the track and pray for Jan and another racing driver, named Bubby Jones.

The message was, "Something's going to happen, and they need prayers."

They followed instructions. Bubby Jones, running third,

also smacked into Parsons's car, but came out with only a bruised knee.

One of the sisters climbed the separating cyclone fence, and moved through the crowd around Jan. Another driver, John Coogan, stood over Opperman, lying in a pool of blood coming from a long, deep gash in his neck and from his head. His blue face and glazed eyes made him look like a dead animal. Coogan broke into tears.

The girl said, "Jan needs our help. Let's pray."

Now Jan Opperman had been dead for six or seven minutes. Queenie and Coogan knelt near Jan, praying.

Suddenly he began to move and groan.

"On the way to the hospital, in the ambulance, I was soaked in blood," states Jan. "Under our helmets, we wear what is called a fire sock, to protect us against fire. That was blood soaked, and there was a bad smell in the ambulance. I remember the doctor beside me with the mike to talk to the hospital. He spoke to the driver, 'Go a little slower and more carefully, because this guy is definitely a DOA.' "

Jan sighed to himself, *Oh, wow, that's* me!

He found himself hurting a little and feeling sad that he had had the best car, was probably going to be the winner, which paid $18,000, and instead had come in last—maybe even worse.

And, yet, Jan feels that his worst race was his best, because he learned how to cry, how to have compassion.

Inside the ambulance on the way to the hospital, Jan started asking God what course he could follow to get out of this situation.

An immediate response echoed through his mind, "Be obedient. Do what I say to do."

Jan then thought of a Scripture: "Praise God in all situations. Be joyful in all trials and tribulations."

As the doctor worked on him, Jan started praising God aloud and thanking Him.

"This blew the doctor's mind," Jan relates. "So I really

started praising and thanking Him, and things got better and better, especially when I started praising in my prayer language, or tongues.''

Two people, Queenie and Linda, had prayed in Jesus' name for Jan to be brought back to life, and so it was.

''They rolled me into the hospital on a gurney,'' explains Jan. ''And they were all ready for surgery on me. They zipped me right up to the brain-scan machine, which was then one of the few in the United States, to find out what damage was done to my exposed brain. They knew it would take instant surgery to give me a chance of survival.

''A bunch of people started praying for me again. They knew that brain surgery is dangerous. When they got me to the brain-scan machine, they no longer found a hole in my skull. There was just a small slit in the skin, and they sewed that up. The brain-scan machine showed absolutely no injury, just that I had had a regular bruise, as if I had been hit in the head, like a football player or fighter, and had just been knocked out. They found no brain damage, nothing to operate on. The doctors were really confused and amazed. You wouldn't believe the looks on their faces. And the big gap in my neck—that had really been bleeding a lot. It was now gone without even a trace of a scar.''

While the doctors who attended Jan Opperman witnessed a single miracle, Dr. William Standish Reed, has witnessed many miracles, including raisings from the dead.

One of the latter happened to his son Rob, then two years old, as reported by Dr. Reed in an interview with Pat Robertson on the Christian Broadcasting Network's 700 Club. Dr. Reed also dealt with this story in his book, *Surgery of the Soul*.

Rob developed pneumonia, unknown to his parents.

''I got up in the morning for surgery and noticed he was still feverish,'' Dr. Reed said. ''When I came back into the room, he didn't look right. He was cyanotic (blue skinned from not enough oxygen in the blood) . . . and I felt for a heartbeat. I didn't have a stethoscope. There was no pulse, no respiration. He was flaccid, limp when I picked him up, and I realized, so far as I could determine, he was dead.

"I cried out to God and pleaded with Him. I was not really a Christian who was close to Jesus at the time. I thought I was serving God completely at that time by being a good surgeon.

"Oh, God, please don't take my little boy from me!"

For ten minutes, Dr. Reed did everything he could think of to help Rob.

". . . As I was praying and weeping before God, I felt life come back into him. He came back to life with no brain damage."

Not long after this, Dr. Reed, practicing in Michigan, performed an operation late one day and heard a request over the loudspeaker for any doctor in the hospital to go to the pediatrics department.

When he arrived there, a nurse handed him a stethoscope and asked if he would go inside and declare dead a little girl who had died four or five minutes before.

The nurse volunteered that a resuscitator had been used on the patient, but she had not responded. Dr. Reed agreed to take care of the matter, go through the formality of putting a stethoscope to her chest, listening, and then signing the chart that she was officially dead.

Standing beside Dr. Reed at the bedside, the little girl's mother looked desolate with grief. The doctor stopped the resuscitator and the IV going into a cut on the girl's left leg.

All at once, Dr. Reed felt he should do more than just give the death pronouncement. He put the stethoscope to his ears and listened. There was no heartbeat. Unquestionably, she was dead. Then, through his mind flashed the drama of several weeks before with his son. So he placed his hand upon the little girl's head thinking:

"You know, it says in the Bible, '. . . these signs shall

follow them that believe; In my name . . . they shall lay hands on the sick, and they shall recover.' That isn't put in the Bible just to fill up space. . . . That's got to be true.''

With his hand on the little girl's head, he prayed, ''Jesus, You gave my little boy back to me. Would You give this little girl back to her mother?''

Then a sound came through the stethoscope.

Her heart had started again! She was back with her mother.

Some years later, Dr. Reed was in California and ran into a Pentecostal preacher from Michigan, who told him, ''You know, Dr. Reed, that little girl who got raised up. Did you know that we were having a prayer meeting in our church for her at that very time?''

Speaking of the girl's return to life, Dr. Reed said, ''You never know how many people are involved in any kind of situation. One of the great things to know is that we're not alone. You can be in Poland or Czechoslovakia, behind the Iron Curtain, as we were, and you just have that sense. You feel the dismal sort of isolation and the hopelessness, but yet, you're sustained by prayer, and you can feel those prayers.''

Prayer does sustain, as Michael Esses, Bible authority and teacher of Anaheim, California, knows. It also can return the dead to life.

Dr. Esses speaks from personal experience on this point. This is the story he told in his book *Michael, Michael, Why Do You Hate Me?*

Some years ago, he, his wife Betty, their son Joel, and one of their two daughters, twelve-year-old Kathy, were vacationing in Ensenada, Mexico. They were relaxing in their trailer in a park where all vehicles are parked on high paved ground, with concrete on the perimeter below. Accidentally, Kathy leaned against the trailer door and plunged to the concrete, eight feet below, landing square on her head, which was split open.

Michael and Betty snatched up a blanket and ran out to help, putting the blanket under her. Immediately it was drenched with blood.

"As I picked up Kathy, I was drenched with blood," said Michael. "We knew she was dead. There wasn't a breath of life in her."

They sent Joel to the next trailer to find out the location of the nearest hospital. He learned that a civil hospital was at the far end of town but that a nearer hospital was the Mexican Hospital of Social Security.

They raced Kathy to the Social Security Hospital emergency room, where she was examined. Doctors found no respiration or heartbeat.

"We're very sorry," a doctor said, "but there's nothing we can do!"

At that very moment, the thought ran through Michael's mind that Jesus is Lord.

Michael immediately turned to Jesus Christ, praying, "Lord, grant me the ability to praise You at this moment when I feel like not praising You. Grant me the ability to praise You in this circumstance. Grant me the faith to trust You for Your word. Grant me the ability not to panic. Just pour a double portion of Your love, Your grace, and Your mercy upon myself, Betty, my son Joel, and my daughter Laurie. As far as we're concerned, Kathy is dead. But her life is in Your hands.

"We know You are the way, the Resurrection, the Truth, the Power."

They then laid hands upon Kathy and prayed. Nothing happened. The government hospital sent them to the Civil Hospital, seven miles away, to get a declaration of death and a death certificate. The hospital received her lifeless body in the examining room. Pretty soon they heard one of the doctors come out, saying, "Loco, Americanos!"

Michael understood that he had said, "Crazy Americans!'' He approached the doctor and asked if he spoke English. The doctor nodded.

"What do you mean by *loco?*" asked Michael.

"Well, you crazy Americans bother us with all sorts of things. There's nothing wrong with your child!''

Flabbergasted, Michael replied, "But we were at the Social Security Hospital, and she was dead when they sent us here!''

The doctor invited Michael and Betty into the examining room, and there was Kathy, sitting up. They had shaved her head where it had been split open. Jesus had resurrected her as he had the daughter of Jairus, the ruler of the synagogue.

"There was not even a scratch on her head," said Michael. "The doctors looked at the blanket, all soaked with blood, and they could not understand it.''

But the Esses family needed no explanation.

Once an almost unheard-of miracle, raising from the dead is occurring more frequently in our times.

Demos Shakarian, president of the Full Gospel Business Men's Fellowship International, with chapters in all parts of the world, has received two reports of this miracle from chapter presidents.

A young man in Jacksonville, Florida was pronounced dead. He had been killed by a thirty-eight-caliber bullet and was ready to be transported to the morgue. He was prayed over by a Full Gospel Business Men's Fellowship director. Within seconds he rose up in bed, completely rational, and asked for water.

A Full Gospel group visited a South African hospital to pray for a sick man. Upon arrival, they learned that he had been dead for so long that a doctor had already made out his death certificate. Over protests of hospital officials, who thought it absurd, they insisted on praying over the man. Within several minutes, he returned to life. The man now carries his death certificate in his breast pocket to verify that he is a modern Lazarus.

And there are more cases of this kind, covering the full range of miracles promised in John 14:12–14—miracles that defy imagination and yet are a matter of record.

One of the most spectacular is that which happened to Dr. Richard E. Eby, of Upland, California. This was related by both the physician and his wife on a Christian Broadcasting Network 700 Club telecast and presented in full, colorful detail in the book *Caught Up Into Paradise*.

Some years ago, Dr. Eby and his wife were in Chicago at the old residence of an aunt. He had filled a large carton with various materials to be carted to a dump and carried it out into the balcony to throw it down to a waiting boy. As he bumped the railing, it gave way, and he plunged headfirst to the concrete.

Mrs. Eby, working three rooms away, heard the sickening thud and rushed to the balcony, instantly seeing Dr. Eby below, his head in a pool of blood, split open, and his scalp down over his ears.

He lay there, gray and still, his brains exposed. Mrs. Eby, a former nurse, let out a scream, which attracted a woman in the home next door, who phoned for an ambulance.

In the emergency room, the neurosurgeon, who had served in Viet Nam for four years, took one look at the patient, and said he had never seen a head like that, even in Viet Nam.

Mrs. Eby prayed a prayer of resignation. "I asked God if it was His will to bring Him back to me. If God didn't have anything for him to do, I asked Him to just take him. If He wanted us to do something for Him with our lives, I asked that He bring him back."

Bleeding had stopped when Dr. Eby reached the hospital. They took him to X ray and then surgery, the latter for four

to six hours. He had started to breathe, but the doctors gave
her no reason for hope. It was just a matter of time for
inevitable death.

At the moment that Dr. Eby had impacted the concrete,
he, a born-again Christian, was transported to paradise.
During his death on earth, he had had a mind staggering and
beautiful experience in heaven.

When he returned to earth and emerged from uncon-
sciousness, the neurosurgeon told him that his brain was
like jelly, that he would be dead in minutes, and that he
should quickly instruct his wife on his business affairs. The
only reason an autopsy hadn't been performed on Dr. Eby
was that they couldn't get consent.

But he didn't die.

Next morning Dr. Eby had 196 stitches in his head.
Paralyzed from the chin down, he could only move his head
a trifle, and, somehow, the bandage came off. Mrs. Eby
states, "I went in at eight o'clock. Those one hundred and
ninety-six stitches were healed, and the doctor was so
frightened he wouldn't touch him. . . . They told me he
would have to have a lot of facial surgery afterward, because there had been a big hole there, but God is the best
facial surgeon."

Today Dr. Eby is completely normal and practicing as
both a physician and surgeon, but he will never get over the
experience he had in heaven the moment his head struck
the pavement.

Dr. Eby told the Christian Broadcasting Network audience that his transfer from earth to heaven was instantaneous: "Faster than the speed of thought. If I tried to explain
it, it would have been done before I could start my sen-
tence."

Asked by host Pat Robertson how long he was in
paradise, Dr. Eby replied, "There are no clocks there. I
instantly realized I was in eternity. When you are in eter-

nity, you feel it. You sense the presence of Jesus in everything you hear, see, smell, touch. It is so fantastic that English can't describe it. And Paul who had the same experience, which he explains in Corinthians twelve, said that it was unutterable for him, and he was a student of Hebrew and Greek . . . ."

Dr. Eby found himself with a new body and mind in heaven, where before you ask questions, you have the answers "like pushing a button for every library in the world." His body was celestial, "Made of most beautiful cloudlike material." There are no bones, muscles, intestines, heart, or lungs.

It is impossible in limited space to describe all the things mentioned by Dr. Eby during the telecast. He spoke of glorious, perfectly symmetrical, ever-fresh flowers, and fragrances more pleasing than any earthly perfume, as well as celestial music: "Ever since my youth, I have had my own orchestra and played instruments, so I know the difference between instruments, vocal, minor, and major. It isn't that kind of music at all. It is heavenly music . . . . It was emanating a little from me, the flowers, the grasses, the trees, and from the skies . . . ."

Anyone who wants a preview of paradise can find it in Dr. Eby's book, *Caught Up Into Paradise*.

13 The Lost Dimension Regained

> "It's something like dewarping
> and dewoofing a rug. All you have
> left is fuzz."

Some years ago, a young, red-haired, scholarly looking fellow named Paul Gray approached me after our charismatic vesper service at the First Reformed Church—the same service visited by Walter Cronkite's crew.

He said he had just graduated from Duquesne University, a Roman Catholic university in Pittsburgh and was preparing to be a professor of theology in the Roman Catholic church. In fact, he went on to be a teacher at Gannon College, a Roman Catholic school in Erie, Pennsylvania.

Just before graduation, his favorite professor invited him to dinner. Over the coffee, he asked, "Paul, what would you say if I were to tell you that the Book of Acts is not only relevant today but normative—that that same dimension of power and joy and glory and love that those first-century Christians enjoyed is available today, and anything less than that is subnormal Christianity? What would you say if I were to tell you our chaplain here and professor So-and-so and I have received the same infilling of the Holy Spirit that Peter, James, John and Mother Mary received on the day of Pentecost?"

The professor continued, "This has so transformed our spiritual life. It's been a door into a whole new dimension of first-century Christianity. And we're yearning to share it with you students.''

So some thirty students met with the professors at a Catholic retreat house known as the Ark and the Dove, a prophetic name.

When the students heard that these professors spoke in tongues, they took a dim view of the whole experience. The retreat was not going well at all. Then one morning a nun came in and said, ''I'm sorry you couldn't get water for your baths. We had a plumber in to check out the system, and he says there's nothing wrong with the system. It's just that the well went dry.''

So the professors thought, *Well, then, we'll call off the retreat. It wasn't going very well anyway. This will be a good excuse. We don't want to inconvenience the nuns further.* But then they looked at it in another way, saying, *How foolish of us! What is the point of this retreat? Isn't it that Jesus Christ is the same yesterday, today, and forever? That He's still doing the same miracles that He did two thousand years ago? If Jesus were here—and He is here—He'd fill this well for us. Here's a chance to de-monstrate this, and we're running from it.*

So, instead of calling off the retreat, they went to the chapel and prayed for Jesus to fill that well. And then they didn't go right in and turn on the faucets to see if He'd answered the prayer. They didn't wait for the manifestation to believe for the fact. ''. . . What things soever ye desire, when ye pray, believe that ye receive them, and ye shall have them'' (Mark 11:24).

By faith alone, they thanked Jesus for filling the well, and then they turned on the faucet, and the water gushed out. In the words of Paul Gray, ''When we saw that water gush from the faucet, a sense of awe came over us as we realized what this meant: that Jesus Christ really was doing the same things today as two thousand years ago. In that moment, every one of us was converted.''

And before they left, all of them had been filled with the Holy Spirit. This was the beginning of the Charismatic Renewal in the Roman Catholic Church. Today Father Scranski, the Superior General of the Paulist Fathers, says that Pentecost is spreading all over the world, nine times faster than any other religious movement.

Now why did God begin that outpouring of the Holy Spirit with a miracle of the well? because we have a God who loves to speak in figures. Where did Jesus first mention the baptism of the Holy Spirit? at a well in Samaria, and He described it in everlasting terms, not as a pump that needed to be primed, but an artesian spring, a spring of living water. And this is the difference the baptism of the Holy Spirit makes. It changes a pump-priming Christian into a spring-well Christian.

The typical Christian is like a pump that needs to be primed. He needs to be primed to witness, primed to read the Word of God, primed to worship, primed to do all the things he should do spontaneously, out of the fullness of his heart; but in this experience, God puts artesian wells of praise, worship, and thanksgiving down in the depths of our beings, and it's springing up in praise, worship, and witness.

All of us have the potential of being granted one or more of the marvelous gifts of the Holy Spirit, ranging from speaking in tongues (a foreign language unknown to us) to the gift of miracles.

The beginning of these gifts is faith, belief in the Word of God as written, not as subtracted from by the finite mind of man. I know this is true, because I have been there. Trained in an orthodox Lutheran seminary, I always had the vague feeling that many glorious scriptural promises of God had been eroded away by man.

The reason we have modernism is really because higher critics in theological seminaries decided that miracles are scientifically impossible. If they are impossible, they could never have happened, even in the Bible. To make the Bible relevant to the mind of modern man, they must go back and carefully delete the supernatural, anything that smacks of the miraculous; they do not explain it, but explain it away.

What they call it is demythologization of the Scriptures. It's something like dewarping and dewoofing a rug. All you have left is fuzz.

Knowing in my innermost depths that there was more to miracles—to the gifts of the Holy Spirit—than the fuzz, I attended an Assemblies of God camp meeting at Green Lane, Pennsylvania, where I saw so many faces and eyes filled with light and love that it seemed like the Promised Land. I saw the raising of hands heavenward and heard the uninhibited praising of the Lord and the speaking in tongues and interpretations.

I was soon aware how bored I was with prayer and how bored God must be.

Suddenly I took my soul by the scruff of the neck and said, "Lord, if it gives You any satisfaction or joy, I'll praise You until I drop."

The moment I abandoned all thought of personal comfort, I found myself entering into a new dimension in which I was being borne along as if Someone were praying through me.

God gave me such a glimpse of His glory that my worship became involuntary. It seemed as if I saw a large reservoir of limpid, pure water, while all around was a huge, parched wilderness and desert. It seemed as if that water was yearning to burst its dikes to beautify that desert.

But there was one bottleneck, and that was Harald Bredesen—not my sins or my vices—just Harald Bredesen, seeking to realize himself and at the same time seeking to serve God. I said, "Jesus, make me after Thine own heart!"

The next morning in the service there came a glorious message in tongues with interpretation. The Lord said to us: "Oh, My people, if you could only stand where I stand and see this world hurtling toward destruction, littered with broken, wounded hearts! I yearn to pour the healing balm of My Gospel into these hearts, but to do so, I must have channels, human channels, completely yielded and surrendered to Me. Will you not yield? Oh, will you not yield?"

There was such yearning in that voice that, for the first time in my life, I realized that the thing that breaks the heart of the Lord is not so much the sins of sinners, but the satisfaction of saints—that we are satisfied in having so little of Him and in His having so little of us!

In that moment, I caught a glimpse of the love of Christ, as He yearned to possess me utterly. My gratitude to Him for His love and wanting me was so great that it was unutterable. I could only say, "Thank You, Jesus. Thank You, Jesus!"

And my hands suddenly rose in awe and wonder. Immediately, as if a bottle within me had uncorked, my real and innermost being that had always been inarticulate was given a voice. A torrent of words poured out in a tongue that I had never heard before.

I thought, "Lord, if this language is from You, then reveal to me what it is. I'm going to walk in the woods."

As I walked in the woods, still speaking in this language, I was met by a little girl, eleven years old, and she looked up at me laughingly saying, "Why, you're speaking Polish!"

I was afraid to speak to her in English for fear I would never again be able to speak in tongues, so I wrote on a piece of paper, which I handed her, "Where is there a Polish man? I want to speak to him."

She led me to a man standing on the stoop of his cabin. The moment I saw him, I said inwardly, "I have never seen this man before, but in Christ, we are brothers!"

And he cried out to me, "In Polish you are saying we are brothers."

Why speak in tongues? As a medium of prayer, intercession and worship. Some years ago Dr. Robert de Haan, famed Christian psychologist, gave me an excellent reason why God gives us a special language for communicating with Him in the Spirit. He had visited with me for a few days to study the deeper work of the Holy Spirit in the subconscious mind.

Later a Reformed Church pastor wrote him, "I understand that you have spent time with Harald Bredesen. What do you make of him psychologically? Is he mentally sound or not?"

Dr. de Haan wrote him back a wonderful letter vouching for my sanity. And then he went on to say, "As a psychologist, I have no explanation for the gift of tongues, but as a Christian I have a theory: We have so contaminated our human speech by the uses to which we have put it that God must give us a brand new language, pure and undefiled, as a worthy vehicle of our worship and praise."

In many cases, tongues is a new and heavenly language or one of tens of thousands of languages, modern or ancient, beyond the knowledge of the most erudite philologists; it is also one which has never been studied by the person praying. Let me give a personal example.

I received a letter from a student at the University of London saying, "I am an Anglican and a convinced Christian. For my doctoral thesis, I have chosen the subject of glossalalia. However, for my professors to take this paper seriously, I must have a firsthand account of a native of a particular country hearing someone speaking his or her language while praying in tongues."

I was impressed by the evident sincerity of his request, and my heart cried out for the kind of evidence that he needed. On that very night God gave me the evidence this man required.

I was speaking in a church in Monterey Park, California, at a meeting set up by Tommy Nickel, editor of *Testimony* magazine. After the service, people crowded into the large prayer room. The whole, wide front row was occupied by candidates for the baptism of the Holy Spirit. After instructing them, I laid hands on each of them, in turn, and briefly prayed in tongues for him or her. Immediately he or she received the baptism.

Meanwhile, in the last row, with her head tilted back against the wall as if in deep prayer, was a woman with a very lovely face. Suddenly she opened her eyes and, obviously excited, beckoned me.

"Are you a native of Serbia?" she asked.

"Why do you ask?"

"Because I happen to be. While I was praying with my eyes closed, suddenly I heard someone speaking in my own native Serbian and saw that it was you. As you laid hands on each person, you spoke the words, 'Na za Boza dajh.' "

"What does that mean?"

"Now Lord, give. Now Lord, give."

"Would you put that into writing?"

"I most certainly will."

The next day I fired her letter off to the doctoral candidate at the University of London. He wrote me back, almost by return mail. "Praise God, this is exactly the evidence that I needed."

Often I am asked if it is uncommon for a person to be able to speak in tongues in more than one language which he or she has never studied.

No. God gives us the abilities we need under various circumstances.

Let me offer illustrations from the life of Bud Godby, a born-again-Christian rider in the rodeo circuit from Denver to Houston, and from my own life.

On one occasion Godby made a trip to Montana with his son and two horses. Heading back for home, he felt led to stop in Arco, Idaho, at the local rodeo arena to present

God's message of salvation to the elderly caretaker there.

"I turned my horses loose to exercise in the arena while I sat in the grandstand talking with the caretaker; my son was playing nearby," says Godby. "We talked for some time, but he kept changing the subject from spiritual matters to rodeos, horses, and events of the past.

"He didn't speak English very well, having come from the old country, so I felt that the language difficulty was a barrier. After an hour or so, I felt I should start home and went to the arena to catch and load my horses. I kept thinking that if the Lord would just give me the ability to speak this man's language I could present the Gospel to him in a way that he would accept Christ.

"I tried to dismiss this as being too 'far out,' but I kept remembering the many different languages the Spirit had given me when praying in the Spirit. After loading the horses, I got a pamphlet on salvation from the car and went back to leave it with the caretaker. Still thinking how effective it would be if the Spirit would enable me to speak to this man in his own language, I sent my boy to put a bucket in the trunk of the car to keep him out of hearing, should God perform this strange act. But my boy was back almost immediately and stood watching what took place next.

"At that moment, my heart was suddenly filled with love and compassion of the Lord, and I began to speak to the old caretaker in a language I didn't understand. Immediately, his face lit up, and he began to say, 'Si! Si!' As I continued speaking, he responded in the same language. His statements or questions were brief, whereas mine were lengthier.

"Tears came to both our eyes, and when we were finished, I tried to explain to him that the Holy Spirit had been speaking to him, but he kept saying admiringly, 'You speak very good Spanish.'

"When I asked him what I had said, he told me I had talked of God and the Bible. I asked if I had said that Jesus had died for our sins, was buried, and rose again after three days. 'Si. Si.' he answered. 'You just got through saying that.'

"How thrilled I was as I realized the Holy Spirit had caused me to cross this language barrier so that He could testify to Christ! The caretaker grabbed me by the coat, and now he only wanted to talk about Jesus. As we left him, I realized that if we didn't meet again at the Arco Rodeo Arena, we would meet in heaven.

"As we drove on toward home, I began to figure out a way to explain to my little boy what he had just seen taking place. I figured it was pretty strong meat for an older Christian, let alone for a child. Just when I had figured out what to say, Dyrk spoke: 'Daddy, Jesus always knows just what to say, doesn't He?' "

That He does, as I learned in a dramatic manner a number of years ago.

I had attended a breakfast in the dining room of New York's Prince George Hotel and returned to the lobby, where I had left my hat on a lounge chair.

In that very chair, instead, was a beautiful, young, olive-complexioned woman.

Suddenly I felt an irresistible urge to talk to her and learned that she was an Egyptian heiress who had to come to New York City to settle an estate. She was friendly, yet a person one could not move in on hurriedly. Still I began thinking, *It would be great if this belle of Mohammedan society could return to Egypt aglow as a witness for Jesus.*

But how to bring up the subject to someone from such a different culture, religion—someone so worldly and sophisticated?

It was like being outside the walls of Jericho without a trumpet. But I had something far greater than a trumpet: prayer.

"Lord," I silently prayed, "I'm at a dead end. I can't

reach her. If You want her, *You're* going to have to do it."
   In that instant, I was astonished to hear myself saying,
"Have you heard this language before?"
   I began to worship the Lord in a rush of strange words.
She seemed stunned, then blurted, "Where did *you* learn
archaic Arabic?"
   "Quick! Write down what I'm saying; then I'll tell you."
   She did what I asked, commenting, "We usually laugh at
the accent of those who study Arabic for years. Yet you
have no accent. You sound like a Bedouin saying his
prayers. You must have been born in Egypt."
   "No!" I read her parts of the sixteenth chapter of Mark:
"And these signs shall follow them that believe, In my
name . . . they shall speak with new tongues."
   "Do you believe this?"
   "Yes, I do. I'm an Egyptian, but not a Muslim. I'm a
Catholic of the ancient Uniate Rite. My mother loved Jesus.
She was always talking about Him, though much to my
embarrassment. Since she died two years ago, I've come to
see how desperately I need what she had. I've found it on
the outside, but inside," she pointed to her heart, "I'm cold
and dead. Can you tell me how to make it happen here?"
   I shared Jesus with her and then with her sister, who
joined her.
   Oh, how my heart leaped that the power of the Holy
Spirit had brought me together with this lovely woman so
that I could introduce her to Jesus.

   How does one go about realizing the gifts of the Spirit?
Bud Godby tells how he did it.
   "As I continued to study the Scriptures, I found that
Spirit-filled believers had access to certain gifts: nine, in
fact. I found a treasure in First Corinthians 12:1: 'Now
concerning spiritual gifts, brethren, I would not have you
ignorant.' And then in First Corinthians 14:1: 'Follow after
charity, and desire spiritual gifts . . . .'

"Realizing that I was to desire these gifts, and God didn't want me to be ignorant about them, I began to read about them. I found them listed as the word of wisdom, the word of knowledge, the gift of faith, gifts of healing, the working of miracles, prophecy, discerning of spirits, divers kinds of tongues, and interpretation of tongues.

"I went directly to the Lord. I prayed, 'Now Lord, I asked You to save me, and You did. I asked You to fill me with the Holy Spirit, and You did. Now, I want all nine of these gifts!'

". . . Under many different circumstances, the Lord has brought into operation through me seven of the nine gifts of the Holy Spirit. I am confident that, should the need arise, He would give me the faith to operate in the other two for His glory, for it has been well said, 'He is more willing to give than we are to receive.' "

As Bud Godby found, we must ask Jesus for the gifts of the Holy Spirit and then appropriate them in order to receive them.

The miracle of the well that launched the Catholic Charismatic Renewal movement is a living parable about receiving the baptism of the Holy Spirit. The water is a symbol of the Holy Spirit. We are the well that needs to be filled. And so in childlike faith we ask Jesus to fill us with the Spirit. We do not wait for any feeling, any sign, any manifestation whatsoever. We believe that He has kept His word. And His word is, ". . . how much more shall your heavenly Father give the Holy Spirit to them that ask him?" (Luke 11:13.) His word is that He will baptize with the Holy Spirit and fire. In every one of the four Gospels, He is introduced as the One who will baptize with the Holy Spirit and with fire. It takes no more faith to believe in Jesus Christ as your Baptizer than it does to believe in Him as your Lamb of God.

When I lead a soul to Christ, I usually use Revelation 3:20, and after the person has asked Jesus Christ to come into his heart, I don't turn to him and say, "Do you feel any different?" or, "Do you feel anything?" No, because that focuses his attention on his feelings, on manifestations, and faith is just taking Jesus at His word. I say to him, "Jesus Christ said if you would open the door, He would come in. You have opened the door, so is He in."

To ask Jesus Christ to baptize you with the Holy Spirit and really mean it, and then not to believe that He has baptized you, is not to doubt yourself, but to doubt *Him.*

In the Word of God there are many promises which used to baffle and frustrate me. One is Mark 11:24, where Christ tells us when we pray for something that He has specifically promised, we are to believe not that He shall give it to us, but that *He has given it to us.* ". . . believe that ye receive them and ye shall have them." This used to seem to me a contradiction of tenses. But this is standard business practice. Let us say that I sign over to you a title to the island of Inaqua. When does Inaqua becomes yours? When you have docked your yacht there? When you have snorkeled in its waters? When you have breathed its spicy breezes? No, Inaqua becomes yours the moment you take title to it. Those Catholic students took title to that full well the moment they thanked Jesus by faith that He had filled that well. And this is what you must do. Now pray this prayer, and instead of waiting for evidence, appropriate the answer by faith, and thank Him and praise Him that He has answered.

"Heavenly Father, I thank Thee for eternal life. Jesus, Thou art my Saviour. Be my Baptizer. Fill me with Your fullness. I yield unto Thee my body, soul, and spirit. I yield Thee my tongue, my most unruly member, which no man can tame. Rule it and tame it as evidence of the fact that Thou hast ruled and tamed me. I've contaminated my human speech by the uses to which I have put it. Give me a whole new language, pure and undefiled, a worthy vehicle of Your worship and praise. Jesus, You say in Your Word

that when I pray for a gift that You have expressly promised, I should believe that I have received it. I have prayed
for the fullness of Your Spirit, and now I take title to it by
faith. I appropriate it with thanksgiving. Thank You, Jesus,
thank You, Jesus, that You have already filled me with Your
Spirit. Amen."

Now that your well has been filled, you have the privilege
of turning on the faucet. Notice I say that it is your privilege
to turn on the faucet. You must exercise the privilege to let
the miracle of the well happen to you.

14 The Greatest Miracle Can Be Yours

> "I had so many bodyguards that nobody could have gotten through the dressing room to tell me about God, so God came into the dressing room and told me about Himself."

Wouldn't it be great if at the center of this cold, hard universe there was a warm, loving heart, and if you knew beyond a shadow of doubt that that heart beat for *you?*

Wouldn't it be wonderful if you knew that the same mind which first planned and now administers the cosmos had a plan for you—a plan that could engage your full potential as a person and cram your life with satisfaction and fulfillment beyond your fondest dreams?

Wouldn't it be exciting if the power that created and sustains the mightiest star and the tiniest molecule were available to you wherever, whenever, and however you needed it?

Well, all of these things are true.

The greatest miracle of all is available to you, merely for the asking—a personal relationship with the Creator of it all.

It may seem amazing, but He yearns to have a close and joyous love relationship with you.

Isn't that the most exciting, life-transforming news you've ever heard? And the beautiful bonus of this intimate relationship is something almost unbelievable: a new birth and the gift of eternal life. The impossible is possible. *You* can live forever. The Scriptures say so plainly:

> Jesus answered and said unto him [Nicodemus], Verily, verily, I say unto thee, Except a man be born again, he cannot see the kingdom of God.
>
> John 3:3

> Behold, I stand at the door, and knock: if any man hear my voice, and open the door, I will come in to him, and will sup with him, and he with me.
>
> Revelation 3:20

Jesus wants to make you alive spiritually so that you can see, hear, perceive, and relate to God in a whole new, intimate, loving, joyous way. Just as you received physical life through physical birth, you receive spiritual life through spiritual birth, the experience Jesus called being born again.

No matter how young or how old you are, you don't know how many heartbeats you have left. No one does. That is why it is important to make a decision for Christ before the last heartbeat. The sooner the better.

God allows us free will. There is no arm twisting. We are free to accept Him or not. Acceptance means we have God's guarantee of life and happiness in heaven with Him. Rejection means eternity in hell.

Is heaven real? Is hell real?

The answer is *yes* to both questions. First, we know this from the Bible, and, second, from ordinary persons who have died, had a preview of paradise or of hell, and come back to verify that what the Bible says is true.

There is one way to be assured of heaven and only *one* way: through acceptance of Jesus Christ, the Son of God, as Lord and Saviour. His death on the cross and His resurrection guarantee us eternal life, but we still have to play our part in this miracle. We must take action. We must accept Him, for ". . . no man cometh unto the Father, but by me" (John 14:6).

For much of his life, former world heavyweight boxing champion George Foreman believed in God but thought he could bypass Jesus and go direct. He learned the hard way that God sent Jesus to earth as His Representative to pay for our sins with His blood to cleanse us so that we can go to heaven.

Something strange happened to George Foreman in a steamy dressing room in San Juan, Puerto Rico.

He lost a fight but, even more important, he almost lost his life on earth, and his chance for eternal life.

George had always thought that so long as you treated others all right, you were okay and were going to heaven.

Although being a loving person is important, it is not the key to salvation.

Up to that time, George only *believed* that Jesus is the Son of God. Now he *knows*.

In the dressing room, he began to pace up and down to cool off, the same as usual, but then, as he thought about the fight, something peculiar happened.

The word *death* intruded into his mind, and kept drumming louder and louder: death, death, *death,* until there was no room in George Foreman's mind for anything but *death!*

He was going to die!

George Foreman began to tremble.

Then he heard a voice saying, "George, if you believe in God, why are you so scared to die?"

He replied, "I believe all right, but not enough to die. I still have money, and I can make charitable contributions and tell a lot of people about You. But, God, I don't have to die!"

"George, I don't care about your money," God said. "I want *you!*"

They laid Foreman on the dressing-room table and tried to soothe him, "Champ, don't worry about losing the fight. You can always win another."

"Who's worried about the fight? I'm fixing to die."

At that instant, George was plunged into a dark place.

"I'm sure it was hell," says Foreman. The blackness crowded in on him, and he began to shout, "If this is hell, I don't care. I still believe in God!"

Instantly he was snatched up from the dark place into a place of light.

In the dressing room, he started screaming, "That's all right. I'm dying, but I'm dying for God."

George had always believed in God, but he had avoided references to Jesus in the Bible. He felt, "Jesus Christ is just not for me."

Again he was aware of being on the dressing-room table, struggling, with several men holding him down as the doctor examined him.

"I told the doctor to move back, because the thorns on his head were making me bleed," says Foreman. "I felt blood running down my face, I moved my hands, and there was blood on them and on my feet.

"I started screaming, 'Jesus Christ is coming to life.' I jumped up off the table. I screamed to one of my brothers, 'Jesus Christ is coming to life.' And he replied, 'I know it, and you're not clean enough.'

"I jumped off the table and ran into the shower. That's the worst thing an athlete can do, get into a cold shower. I was yelling, 'Hallelujah, I've been born again.' I had never said anything like that before in my life.

"As I came out of the shower, something from the bottom of my stomach started taking over, and I began talking uncontrollably. Scriptures came out of my mouth. I started speaking in tongues, and they rushed me to the hospital."

An ambulance with siren screaming rushed Foreman to a

hospital, where he was given X rays and a whole battery of tests. He checked out perfectly.

George Foreman left Puerto Rico the happiest man in the world. He said he was "kind of confused, but happy."

Then he began to follow the pattern of most persons who are born again. Foreman became skeptical about his experience and then began to doubt.

"I tried to shake off my whole experience," says George. "After all I intended to be world champion again, famous and rich. I had no intention of spending the rest of my life just carrying a Bible around!"

Foreman got in touch with Dr. Robert Schuller, pastor of Garden Grove Christian Church in California, and told him about his experiences, asking for his opinion.

Dr. Schuller explained that he had not only studied theology but also psychology and psychiatry. After hearing the story, Dr. Schuller told Foreman he believed in the validity of his experience, and he invited George to appear on his nationwide *Hour of Power* television program.

Foreman has given up boxing.

"In boxing, I was just trying to exalt the name of George Foreman. Now I am spending my whole life to exalt the name of Jesus Christ," he says.

He still marvels at the miracle which God worked in his life.

"I had so many bodyguards that nobody could have gotten through the dressing room to tell me about God, so God came through the dressing room and told me about Himself."

Now that he has hung up his boxing gloves, what is George Foreman doing? The most important work in the world: that which helps people to find heaven. He says, "All I want to do is tell people about Jesus. I wouldn't want *anyone* to get down to the last breath, thinking that just because he's been a good person, he's automatically going to heaven."

He believes that there's one way, and only one, to salvation, "You have to come to heaven by Jesus, the Son of God."

George Foreman feels that. God personally gave him a special mission in life. "Because God thought enough of me to reveal Himself to me, I'm going to help reveal Him to others. There are so many people who leave this world who don't even know for a fact that Jesus Christ is the Son of God. Therefore, I'll spend my life telling them."

He also tells that God's Word, the Bible, is the most important reading in his life, although it wasn't always. "I once thought the Bible was a book written by some sheepherders. I couldn't understand the *wherefores* or anything. Now it's my daily food."

In the ring, George Foreman has thrown some hard smashes at the heads and bodies of opponents. Now he's throwing spiritual punches at the hearts of everybody he meets.

One of his most effective is this, ". . . whosoever shall call on the name of the Lord shall be saved . . ." (Acts 2:21).

While those of us in basically Christian nations are free to experience rebirth at no personal risk, individuals in certain countries can do so only under the threat of death.

One person who valued eternal life more than life on earth and made her decision in faith is Madame Bilquis Sheikh, daughter of a prince, whose Muslim family dates back seven centuries in Pakistan history. She tells her story in her book, *I Dared to Call Him Father.*

Some years ago, Madame Sheikh, wife of a former general and minister of the interior, felt she had come to a dead end in the Muslim faith. She met many Christians in governmental circles—kings, princes, ambassadors, and other foreign officials—but none of them ever so much as mentioned their faith to her.

She knew nothing about Jesus Christ and suddenly began to thirst for information about Him. She found that no library or shop had a Bible. Finally, her Christian chauffeur borrowed one for her.

Completely captivated by it, she read incessantly for several days. One night she left the Bible on her bedstand, went to sleep, and had a dream which she couldn't understand.

Soon after, she had a second inexplicable dream. It was unusual for her to dream at all. In the first one, she was standing on a holy mountain, near a crossroads, informing John the Baptist that Jesus had stayed in her home for two days and that they had eaten dinner together and talked. She was about to follow Jesus when she awakened, still feeling the serenity and holiness of the ground on which she had stood.

A strong feeling impressed her that the dream was from God, directing her to Christ.

With a severely limited knowledge of the Bible, it was even harder for her to understand the second dream.

A perfumer had come to her home. She tried one of his samples and said, "Give me this one, and I won't have to look for French perfumes anymore."

The man handed her a second perfume in a dish, telling her to put it on her bedstand and that its fragrance would spread.

Upon awakening, she found her Bible where the dish of perfume had been placed and wondered whether there was a connection between the perfume and the Bible. Her dreams so intrigued her that she had to have answers from somebody who knew the Bible and, although Muslims and missionaries don't mix, she called at the home of Reverend and Mrs. David Mitchell and, without preliminaries, told Mrs. Mitchell about her dreams and asked who John the Baptist was.

Mrs. Mitchell explained that he was the forerunner to

Jesus Christ, the one who baptized with water. Before leaving, Madame Sheikh asked if there is anything in the Bible
connecting Bible reading with perfume.

Mrs. Mitchell told her to read 2 Corinthians 2:14 in the
Living Bible:

> But thanks be to God! For through what Christ has
> done, he has triumphed over us so that now wherever we
> go, he uses us to tell others about the Lord and to spread
> the Gospel like a sweet perfume.

Through one of God's coincidences, she met a Catholic
nun who was a medical doctor, and Madame Sheikh explained that she was in search of God but still was confused
between the Bible and the Koran.

"I told her I had a great desire to find God, no matter the
consequences," Madame Sheikh says.

"I advise you to pray and ask God to show you the right
way," she replied. "Pray to God as if He were your father.
Ask Him to show you the way."

Although Madame Sheikh got on her knees, she could not
bridge the Muslim gulf between herself and a great, faraway
God.

Next morning, with more courage, she tried again, pictur-
ing God as her earthly father, who had never been too busy
to answer her questions.

"My Father," she said and suddenly sensed His presence everywhere in the room. "I felt His love and compassion surrounding me. I felt His eyes of love looking at
me . . . . I felt bathed in an ocean of love.

"Father, if You show me the right way, I will follow You,
whether it's difficult or easy.

"If God wanted me to become a Christian, it would mean
that I would become a social outcast to my family, whom I
loved very much. I could remember only one Muslim who
had become a Christian, who had not been killed—a person

who, for more than twenty years, had been a servant to a missionary. He could never leave the missionary, or he would be killed by Muslims. The unforgivable sin, for the Muslim, is believing in Jesus Christ as the Son of God."

Madame Sheikh asked God's guidance through her Bible reading, and, as she paged through, a passage leaped out at her from the Book of Revelation: chapter 3, verse 20: "Behold, I stand at the door, and knock: if any man hear my voice, and open the door, I will come in to him, and will sup with him, and he with me."

Then the significance of her first dream came to her. Jesus was the way!

Madame Sheikh fell to her knees, praying, "Lord, You don't have to stand outside knocking, for every door of my heart and my home is open to You."

Electricity ran through her entire body.

"Time stood still, and I felt lifted up into heaven . . . ."

When Madame Sheikh later was baptized, word of her action spread through the city. Her family descended upon her, pleading that she stop speaking of Jesus Christ. But she held her ground.

She had no intention of hurting them, but she was aware of a particular passage of the Bible, which she quoted. She showed them that Jesus said:

> Whosoever therefore shall confess me before men, him will I confess also before my Father which is in heaven. But whosoever shall deny me before men, him will I also deny before my Father which is in heaven.
>
> Matthew 10:32, 33

The visitors left sorrowfully, knowing that Madame Sheikh had one thing to look forward to: death.

"Tell my friends not to worry. If I die by bullet wounds, throttling, or knifing, it will be only because the Lord permits it."

As she mentioned the word *knifing,* she trembled with

fright, because she knew she was a physical coward. After her visitors had left, she fell to her knees to pray for protection.

A friend suggested that she put bars on her windows, but she refused. If she did that, it would be an admission of fear and that she didn't trust Jesus. She went to bed in complete peace.

"Around eleven o'clock, I was awakened by a sound outside my window," she says. "I looked out, and my garden was lighted so brightly that I could see it in the smallest detail: every blade of grass, even the petals fallen to the ground. No one could have hidden in the bushes without being seen, the light was so revealing."

The Lord had provided her a miracle light of His protection.

A short time later, she was invited to the United States to offer her Christian testimony in churches, at Christian men's and women's organizations, military bases, and on university campuses.

She is now spreading God's Word as the fragrance of the perfume in her dream spread.

Although the born-again experiences of Madame Sheikh, George Foreman and Melvin Purvis, Jr., were both electrifying and thrilling, can they be considered typical? No.

Yours could be as dramatic as lightning or so subtle that you feel nothing and sense no immediate change. But remember that the object of your action is salvation and a close relationship with the Lord, not thrills.

Some persons make the mistake of using their sense impressions or emotions to confirm whether or not they have actually received Christ. This need not happen to you. Jesus made solemn and unbreakable promises to you in the Bible. Count on His promises, rather than on your sensations or feelings.

If your born-again experience was low-key, be prepared

for Satan, the master at eroding faith. He will work to convince you that this marvelous event in your life didn't happen.

Hold onto your faith!

Do you know what steps to follow to have perfect assurance that you will be born again, have a love relationship with Jesus, and life everlasting? It's very simple. You can do it in your own words (after all, He doesn't stand on ceremony), or you can use the words provided at the end of this chapter.

Before saying anything, you must be genuinely sorry for your sins and then ask Jesus to forgive you and to come into your heart. Then you must tell somebody that you made a decision for Christ.

You can start right now!

God has given you the power of free will and decision. You can say *yes* to Jesus and set in motion the greatest miracle of all times: eternal life.

Ask and you shall receive!

How To Receive Christ

Just say and mean: "Jesus, I am sorry for my sins. Come into my heart and life. Cleanse me. Make me the kind of person You want me to be. Amen."

Share Your Miracle!

If you have experienced a miracle, why not share it with those around you and also with me?

I have plans to follow *Need A Miracle?* with another book on this subject.

So if you have had a miracle, please write me about it and let me know what documentation you have to prove your experience—newspaper or magazine clippings or names of reputable persons for verification: your minister or your physician.

Remember, my interest is not only in physical healings but in the full range of miracles presented in this book—and more.

Harald Bredesen
Charisma Ministries
P.O. Box 2264
Escondido, CA 92025